GETTING IT ACROSS

Tom Cahill SVD

Getting It Across

REFLECTIONS ON THE SUNDAY READINGS OF THE THREE-YEAR CYCLE

the columba press

First published in 2011 by
the columba press
55A Spruce Avenue, Stillorgan Industrial Park,
Blackrock, Co Dublin

Cover by Bill Bolger
Origination by The Columba Press
Printed in Ireland by Gemini International Limited

ISBN 978 1 85607 734 7

Contents

Foreword

Some bits of advice stay with you, some don't. This bit stayed with me: to preach well have a bible in one hand and a newspaper in the other. The reflections in this book come from God's word in scripture and news items in newspapers for the most part.

They come also from an invitation to write a monthly column for *Intercom*. My task was to come up with short reflections on the weekly Sunday Mass readings that would have an unusual focus. I called the column 'Deep End.' Most, but not all, of the reflections in this book have been published in *Intercom* as 'Deep End' pieces.

They are intended as springboards for preachers to dive in at the deep end and listen to God's word with an attentive ear, an open mind and a receptive heart. After plunging, who knows what they may surface with? God's word, ever ancient ever new, should never bore, have a high-yawn factor, or be sanctimonious babble. If the preached word doesn't inspire, challenge, surprise and – yes – even entertain; if it doesn't make us gasp in disbelief, scratch our head in bewilderment, put an ache in our heart for God and love in our heart for each other; and, if it doesn't prise open our mind to things invisible and quicken our pulse to the seduction of eternity, then we haven't been listening to the Word, but merely hearing words.

These short reflections are not only for the Eucharistic banquet. They're food for thought, for prayer both private and in community. And they're a 'serial' for breakfast. Have one with your cornflakes. Why not? They're far more nourishing.

THE SEASON OF ADVENT YEAR A

FIRST SUNDAY OF ADVENT

Readings: Isaiah 2:1-5; Romans 13:11-14; Matthew 24:37-44

Microscope, telescope, horoscope

In his book *God is not Great,* Christopher Hitchens, with near messianic fervour puts mankind on notice: keep to the straight and narrow of scientific exactitude when accepting anything as fact. Otherwise, God forbid (Oops, sorry!), you might end up thinking that there is more to life than science. And that, most certainly, would damage your health.

Really? Just what does science have to offer when it comes to understanding life? I don't mean the nature of living things or inanimate objects. I mean the why of it all. But then, *why* is not a scientific question. Does that mean we shouldn't ask it, or if we do that we shouldn't expect a worthwhile answer? I hope not.

So let's ask it: Why is there anything at all? Science, where art thou? ... Okay, let's change tack. How about the *how* question: How will the universe end? Here science can indicate a distant, if frighteningly feasible scenario: a frozen lifeless waste.

Give me instead the follow-up to what today's gospel describes. After the Second Coming, the New Heaven and New Earth.

Even were it sheer fantasy, let me die aglow with its promise than be numbed lifeless by the eternal emptiness of scientific scenarios.

SECOND SUNDAY OF ADVENT

Readings: Isaiah 11:1-10; Romans 15:4-9; Matthew 3:1-12

Beauty or the Beast?

Thomas Merton writes in *The Ascent to Truth*: 'One of the paradoxes of our age, which has so far not distinguished itself as an Age of Faith, is that millions of men who have found it impossible to believe in God have blindly submitted themselves in human faith to every charlatan who has access to a printing press, a movie screen, or a microphone. Men who cannot believe in the revealed word of God swallow everything they read in the newspapers.' (p 30)

So how about swallowing what we have in today's first reading: 'The nursing child shall play over the hole of the asp, and the weaned child shall put its hand on the adder's den. They will not hurt or destroy on all my holy mountain; for the earth will be full of the knowledge of the Lord.' What an image!

When will we learn that peace is our natural state? Fighting is foreign. Don't believe it? Then what does being made in the image of God mean? What we see is what we get. If we see people as brutes, then brutes they may become.

The earth will be full of the knowledge of the Lord when we are.

THIRD SUNDAY OF ADVENT

Readings: Isaiah 35:1-6, 10; James 5:7-10; Matthew 11:2-11

A Living Masterpiece

'To be dead is to stop believing in the masterpieces we will begin tomorrow.' So claimed Patrick Kavanagh as cited in John O'Donohue's book, *Eternal Echoes* (p 19). Too good a sentiment to be true, you might think. Well, that depends on how you eye a masterpiece. We can all too easily sell ourselves short. There is more to each of us than meets the eye – especially our own.

Have you ever surprised yourself? Have you ever done something you thought you never could, shown a humanity you didn't know you had, opened to an insight that took your breath away, gone that extra mile exhausted yet finished quite refreshed? And, have you discovered that exquisitely subversive truth that the more you give, the more you realise you have to give?

If so, Isaiah's words today will make sense to you: 'Then the eyes of the blind shall be opened, and the ears of the deaf unstopped, then the lame shall leap like a deer, and the tongue of the speechless sing for joy.' But they will make sense in a way you never dreamed of.

You'll gasp as you grasp that, in fact, they refer to you!

FOURTH SUNDAY OF ADVENT

Readings: Isaiah 7:10-14; Romans 1:1-7; Matthew 1:18-24

The Good News and Comfort Zones

A gem of Cherokee wisdom goes as follows: 'When you were born you cried and the world rejoiced. Live your life so that when you die the world cries and you rejoice.' Christmas, in its own way, confirms that we can do just that. That is what the good news proclaims: death is not the end of everything, but the beginning of something new. Death is our passage to the rejoicing.

Our faith is not for pessimists – unless, that is, to transform them into optimists. Recently I came across an amusing definition of a pessimist as one who feels bad when he feels good for fear he'll feel worse when he feels better. No, our faith is not for those. Our faith instils joy, optimism, hope, vision, and trust. Otherwise, how could it be considered good news?

Some people, it seems, just cannot be happy being happy. They seem to feel there's something wrong with it. God doesn't want us to be happy in this vale of tears. A modern-day spin on this dreary spirituality is the blithely imposed duty to leave our so-called 'comfort zones'.

I say, 'Thanks be to God for them.' Just try living without any of them!

THE FEAST OF THE IMMACULATE CONCEPTION

Readings: Genesis 3:9-15, 20; Ephesians 1:3-6, 11-12; Luke 1:26-38

The God-smile

I've never been able to get my head around the Immaculate Conception, except in the simplest of terms. At its simplest, Mary's immaculate conception means that she had God smiling on her as no human being had ever had before.

Intimacy with God means freedom from sin. How could the God-child come from flesh frowned on by the Father? It's inconceivable. How could God become sinful flesh? He couldn't. Become weak flesh, yes; sinful flesh, no. Is there even such a thing as sinful flesh? As a metaphor, yes; as a reality, no.

The old penny catechism stated that 'because of Original Sin our intellect is darkened, our will is weakened, our passions incline us to evil, and we are subject to suffering and death'. Nothing there about flesh becoming sinful. So, if that notion is in our mind, let's dump it.

Today's feast tells us that God is free to smile as he likes, on whom he likes. When he does, sin goes. Flesh – more infused with divinity than we can comprehend – is, was, and always will be holy.

We too are immaculately conceived – in the mind of God. His the dream, ours the privilege to make that dream come true.

MASS OF CHRISTMAS DAY

Readings: Isaiah 52:7-10; Hebrews 1:1-6; John 1:1-18

The Nativity of Our Lord

'Mind boggling' is an expression that can seem over the top when used too readily – but not when applied to Christmas. The news of God becoming man is heady stuff indeed, but for the Creator and Lord of all things to be born in a stable – well, that is just mind-boggling!

And the mind continues to boggle with today's gospel. It's lofty. It's sublime. It tells of the Word – who was with God in the beginning and through whom all things were made – becoming flesh and being rejected by his own. It's not easy to comprehend. Far easier to face a painting of a baby in its mother's arms. Far easier to face the cherubic countenance of a plaster-cast child in a crib. Far easier to dull the mystery with alcoholic cheer, and programmed goodwill. So much easier, in fact, that we may fail to see the connection between two mind-boggling events: Jesus' birth and his resurrection. Jesus' birth is his gateway to resurrection.

Today we celebrate not just our joy at God becoming man. We thrill at our own birth too – it being the gateway to our resurrection.

Now that's mind-boggling too.

THE HOLY FAMILY

Readings: Sirach 3:2-6, 12-14; Colossians 3:12-21; Matthew 2:13-15, 19-23

Focus on Family

Albert Einstein once said that there were only two ways to live one's life: 'as though nothing is a miracle, or as though everything is'. Better play safe and take the second option – especially when it comes to family.

Family is where we most readily experience the miracle that life is. It's where we fashion ourselves, and are fashioned, as human beings. It's where we learn the art of living, the beauty of words such as 'please' and 'thank you.' It's where we learn to brush teeth, wash hands, and of course to flush. It's where we learn to be on time for meals we haven't had to prepare ourselves, and to help with wash-up instead of running off to play. In short, it's where we learn to think of others and not just of ourselves. It's where we learn eventually what Okakura Kakuzo notes in *The Book of Tea,* that 'those who cannot feel the littleness of great things in themselves are apt to overlook the greatness of little things in others.' (p 6)

Most of these important lessons come courtesy of parents. No wonder then the word of God speaks so highly of them today in Ben Sirach.

Where would we be without them?

SECOND SUNDAY AFTER CHRISTMAS

Readings: Sirach 24:1-2, 8-12; Ephesians 1:3-6, 15-18; John 1:1-18

Wisdom

A Chinese proverb tells us that the first step towards wisdom is getting things by their right names. What more important name to get right than 'God'? So, is our response to that name chilly, wary, or warm? In *Things Hidden,* Richard Rohr points out, 'Most people do not realise that humanity did not, by and large, expect love from God before the biblical revelation.' Capricious pagan gods were to be placated. Those who submitted to them, though intelligent, lacked wisdom in naming them 'gods' instead of 'illusions'.

Our God is not an illusion, or capricious. He's steadfast in love. Made in his image and likeness, so too are we. Any response to him on our part other than love would be unworthy of him. He gives love, wants love; he *is* love.

Today's first reading calls God 'the Most High'. That's where we set our sights: high. We don't lower them to near worship of superficial entertainment, or to escapist busyness that blinds us to the past, locks us to the present, and numbs us to the future. Instead let's use right names and call the past 'teacher', the present 'opportunity', and the future 'hope'.

Then life can bring us wisdom, and fashion us in full. Otherwise, the words of Greek tragedian Aeschylus (525-456 BC) may haunt us by their beauty and their dread: 'Even in our sleep, pain which cannot forget falls drop by drop upon the heart until, in our despair, against our will, comes wisdom through the awful grace of God.'

THE EPIPHANY OF THE LORD

Readings: Isaiah 60:1-6; Ephesians 3:2-3, 5-6; Matthew 2:1-12

All Kinds of Everything

Someone once described love as the ability to see butterflies in caterpillars. I think that holds true for faith too. The feast we celebrate today, the Epiphany, is a good example of that.

Epiphany, a strange sounding word of Greek origin, simply means seeing something, or someone, more clearly than ever before. It's sudden, and it takes your breath away. Something we are very familiar with we suddenly discover has more to it than we thought. Someone we thought we knew inside out suddenly gob-smacks us into seeing that we can't take her, or him, or anyone else for granted – ever. Mystery rules, ok! That's epiphany. We need constant contact with mystery – so life's richness isn't diluted.

After their vision, the three wise men in today's gospel reading have their dream. It warns them to avoid Herod. Some people can't cope with mystery. Their attitude is all wrong, their values are all wrong, they are all wrong. As the wise men avoided Herod, so too must we, with whatever name or in whatever form he may appear. He's the one who tramples on caterpillars and thinks butterflies are for the birds. Clearly, besides mystery we also need our dreams.

THE BAPTISM OF THE LORD

Readings: Isaiah 42:1-4, 6-7; Acts 10:34-38; Matthew 3:13-17

Who? Me!

Asking the right question is as important as getting the right answer. It means we're on the right track to self-understanding. We're clued in to life. We're focused on the present but with our sights on the future too. But, not everybody is. Those who never ask that all-important question 'Who am I?' can't possibly be. As human beings we don't just walk around with mystery every day. We are mystery walking around! The answer to the question, 'Who am I?' is not my name. It has nothing to do with my name. I can change that if I wish. But I can't change my 'who' no matter how much I might wish to do so, because that is immutable before God.

So, I need to meet that 'who', to discover what makes me, me. Is it status, success, money, ability, intelligence? These play their part in forming me, as do failures, limitations and fears, but there's more to me than all of those put together.

I need to ask that all-important question 'Who am I?' and wait patiently until I hear the answer I crave; until – in sheer disbelief – I hear the words spoken to Jesus in today's gospel: 'You are my beloved son/daughter in whom I am well pleased.'

FIRST SUNDAY OF LENT

Readings: Genesis 2:7-9, 3:1-7; Romans 5:12-19; Matthew 4:1-11

Temptation

Oscar Wilde's quip that he could resist everything except temptation contains a grain of wisdom. In a quirky way it's saying: careful how you fight temptation; you may not win. Oscar clearly didn't. Neither did Adam or Eve.

Temptation trades in lies as today's first reading shows. It is countered by truth, as today's gospel shows. When tempted to turn stones into bread Jesus doesn't 'engage' with the temptation. He confronts it with truth: God's word is the source of life, not bread. When Satan tempts him a second time, Jesus warns him not to tempt God. No fear, or indecision there. Satan ignores the warning and tempts Jesus again. His offer of all the kingdoms on earth to Jesus if only he would worship him is so preposterous that Jesus summarily dismisses him. And he goes.

Satan is not as powerful as he would like to be seen to be. While temptation to evil is a fact of life, so too is the victory of good over evil. Evil's power has been definitively defeated. The Incarnation has seen to that.

Evil has a past, and a present, but no future. Neither do those who submit to it.

SECOND SUNDAY OF LENT

Readings: Genesis 12:1-4; 2 Timothy 1:8-10; Matthew 17:1-9

Rainy Sundays

British novelist Susan Ertz (1894-1985) once remarked that millions long for eternity who wouldn't know what to do with themselves on a rainy Sunday afternoon. Nowadays, the lure of unreality and cyberspace, from television and the Internet, has eased that problem to some degree. Unfortunately, in so doing virtual reality increasingly substitutes for the real thing.

Our faith, however, carries us far beyond the confines of cyberspace. It propels us to the edge of eternity. It blows our mind with the promise of resurrection and a fullness of life beyond imagining. And, it does so while keeping our feet firmly fixed on Mother Earth.

The invitation to journey beyond cyberspace and unreality was issued a long time ago to Abraham, as we hear in today's first reading. He is to leave his familiar surroundings and move without knowing his final destination. He will discover that along the way. Trust and commitment come first. Fulfilment of promise comes later.

Sunday afternoons are not a problem for Abraham. He has a mission in life to carry out, a future to face, a destiny to fulfil – hail, rain, or snow. May we use our Sunday afternoons wisely. This Lent may they be times to abstain from the self-indulgence of feeling bored.

THIRD SUNDAY OF LENT

Readings: Exodus 17:3-7; 2 Romans 5:1-2, 5-8; John 4:5-42

Sophisticated Slavery

In his book, *Seeking Spirituality,* Ronald Rolheiser states that the incarnate God is found first and foremost in peoples' homes. According to him 'The God of the Incarnation is more domestic than monastic.'

The Israelites, in today's first reading, don't see God that way. For them, he is external: present in a burning bush, in a pillar of cloud, in a pillar of fire, and on a storm tossed mountaintop. So external is he that they doubt his presence at all in time of difficulty. For them, he is a fair-weather god.

When their basic needs are not met they complain loudly. Forgetful of their recent past of slavery and misery, they bemoan their perilous present and their uncertain future. They want sustenance, security, and comfort. Otherwise they resort to idols for what they want.

Are we – modern and sophisticated, as we like to think – all that different? Don't we too have our idols: consumerism, entertainment, fashion, popularity and image? Aren't we enslaved by the shop-till-you-drop impulse, the must-have craving for the latest fashions and trends – and an insatiable appetite for praise and popularity?

Could we say that our god is not just domestic, but domesticated?

FOURTH SUNDAY OF LENT

Readings: 1 Samuel 16:1, 6-7, 10-13; Ephesians 5:8-14; John 9:1-41

Living with Ambivalence

In *Confronting Power and Sex in the Catholic Church,* Bishop Geoffrey Robinson writes, 'In the *First Book of Samuel* there are two stories of the appointment of Saul as the first king of Israel.' One favours it; one doesn't, thus indicating the Bible's ambivalence towards kingly rule over Israel. He concludes, 'The perfect religious organisation, with the divine and human in total harmony, never has and never will exist.' The same is true for any individual.

Take David in today's first reading. God shows no ambivalence in choosing him as king. But, later David grossly misuses his power to have Bathsheba's husband, Uriah, killed so he can have her for himself. Yet, God does not disown him. God 'does not see as mortals see'. He knows that with the evil there is also much good in David.

We too must live with ambivalence – in ourselves and in others. Black and white may be easier on the eye than grey, but perhaps compassion is best of all. For, as Timothy Radcliffe OP claims in his book, *Sing a New Song,* 'Compassion surely trains the eye to see the loveliness of God in unexpected places.'

FIFTH SUNDAY OF LENT

Readings: Ezekiel 37:12-14; Romans 8:8-11; John 11:1-45

Life-giving

Many years ago I saw a Hollywood 'religious' film about Jesus of Nazareth. Jeffrey Hunter – he of the brilliant blue eyes, for those old enough to remember him – portrayed Jesus. In one scene, the raising of Lazarus to life (today's gospel reading), Hunter calls on him to come forth from his tomb. He does, wrapped in layers of loose cloth, except for his face, which would have been better wrapped too. He looked hideous. I thought that if that was what being raised to life meant, he'd have been better left as he was.

In today's first reading Yahweh says he will bring the house of Israel up from its grave and put his spirit within them so that they live. No ghoulish appearances there, no mummified creatures creaking around zombie-like as in a horror film. God gives his Spirit, beautiful, vibrant, and creative. Whoever opens up to that Spirit, in turn becomes beautiful, vibrant, and creative.

The body is often debased in today's entertainment industry. Constant exposure to that debasement can degrade one's respect for the beauty and sanctity of the human body – the dwelling place of God's Holy Spirit. Nothing debased or second grade ever comes from the hand of God.

PALM SUNDAY

Readings: Isaiah 50:4-7; Philippians 2:6-11; Matthew 26:14-27:66

Palming off Bread

Mahatma Gandhi once said that the only form in which God dare appear to a starving man is in the form of bread. A startling statement indeed! But is it true? Not entirely, because it doesn't go far enough. It stops at the 'incarnation' of bread.

Today's second reading goes all the way. It tells of Jesus, who – though in the form of God – empties himself to become a slave. No salvation from a distance here. Furthermore, the God-man then humbles himself and accepts death on a cross – not to provide a starving man with bread, but to offer him eternal life.

What that reading from Philippians tells us is truly awesome and frightening. It's awesome because it's so up-front about God. Not only does it challenge us to believe in God's existence, it presents that God as so besotted by love for humanity that he becomes one of us – compounding to the Nth degree any difficulties we might have with God's existence in the first place. It's frightening because it doesn't try to make things easy. No half-measures with God. Appearing as bread is comprehensible. But appearing as another starving man is breathtaking.

God became one of us. How closely do we identify with those who starve?

EASTER SUNDAY

Readings: Acts 10:34, 37-43; Colossians 3:1-4; John 20:1-9

Boldly Going

Believing that someone has risen from the dead is quite an achievement. It means that you have freed your mind from the limitations of reason. Human reason is limited, is it not? So, is it not desirable to boldly go where reason alone can't take you? If we never take that step into what is seen as in a glass darkly we will not develop fully. We will be so fearful of appearing gullible, or stupid; so fearful of derision from those considered more 'enlightened' and intelligent, so afraid of drifting into insanity, that we will imprison our mind in shallowness and limit our ability to mature spiritually.

As people of faith we have staked our life on what we believe. If Jesus has not risen then what's the point in seeking 'the things that are above'? What's the point in being a Christian if the highpoint of Jesus' life was a lie, a non-event, a con artist's ruse? Then our faith would be a sham, our values mere delusion.

Look into the eyes of your loved ones: wife, husband, son, daughter, and tell them they have no lasting value. Then see if you can ever look them in the eye again.

SECOND SUNDAY OF EASTER

Readings: Acts 2:42-47; 1 Peter 1:3-9; John 20:19-31

No Doubt About it

In his book, *Sing a New Song*, Timothy Radcliffe OP states: 'But if I speak as someone who knows it all, untroubled by doubt, then people may be very impressed by my knowledge, but they may feel it has little to do with them.' Doubt is more engaging than certainty. Doubt explores. Certainty can't. How can you journey if you've already arrived? Certainty degrades dialogue to monologue. It proselytises instead of evangelises. It stymies communication by making it confrontational, or by short-circuiting it altogether.

Thomas, in today's gospel is a fine example of the doubter feeling his way to belief – quite literally: '... unless I put my finger in the mark of the nails and my hand in his side, I will not believe.' Thomas was comfortable with his disbelief because it was sincere. He had a healthy aversion to accepting the seemingly preposterous.

Many people, especially those in authority, or those considered to be authorities, are uneasy with doubt. Doubt, for them, excludes God's Spirit. It instills fear instead of the thrill of the chase. Doubt means weakness, not potential for growth. One wonders if those who find it difficult to say: 'I don't know', find it any easier to say: 'My Lord, and my God!'

THIRD SUNDAY OF EASTER

Readings: Acts 2:14, 22-23; 1 Peter 1:17-21; Luke 24:13-35

Death: Getting it Right

Resurrection depends on dying – but of the right kind. For there are two: one that brings on death, and one that brings on life. In his book, *The Seed and the Sower,* Laurens van der Post describes the former: 'Death is not something that happens at the end of our life. It is imprisonment in one moment of time, confinement in one sharp uncompromising deed or aspect of ourselves. Death is exclusion from renewal of our present-day selves.'

Sound familiar? Something bad happens and we never free ourselves from its murky memory, or its corrosive touch. In a moment of madness something evil, or stupid is done. That moment must not destroy a life.

The two travellers in today's gospel discover this. A 'moment' of collective madness had killed their Messiah and shattered their world. They could have slumped into despair and cowered in mediocrity. But no! They were dying to their disbelief by pondering news some women had brought that the Messiah was alive. They were dying to their confusion by opening to Jesus' explanation of the scriptures. They were dying to despair in the friendship of breaking bread together. That dying led to their resurrection, their renewal.

And, renewed, they returned immediately to where they had left – no longer afraid of the dark.

FOURTH SUNDAY OF EASTER

Readings: Acts 2:14, 36-41; 1 Peter 2:20-25; John 10:1-10

Life: Full and Free

When I worked in Indonesia as a missionary, a priest friend one day introduced a Chinese friend of his to me in the following manner: 'This is so-and-so. He's not Christian yet, he's still free.' I couldn't believe my ears. How could anyone think that being a Christian limited your freedom! Now, my friend may have thought he was being funny or subtle, but if so it was lost on me.

But his words did strike home. I wonder how many people actually think that religion cramps their style. And I wonder also what such people would want to do that they couldn't do by being a Christian – particularly in the light of today's gospel where Jesus tells us that he has come to bring life in all its fullness.

However, it doesn't come pre-packed. It has to be worked on and worked with. Living as Jesus wants us to, leads to a full life. His Way is a precious gift, not a wearisome burden. It empowers, it doesn't unman. It frees, it doesn't enslave. But all the talk in the world won't convince anybody, if we who are on that Way don't show its fullness in our life through joy, maturity, generosity, courage, and hope.

FIFTH SUNDAY OF EASTER

Readings: Acts 6:1-7; 1 Peter 2:4-9; John 14:1-12

Cornered by the Stone

Today's second reading describes Jesus as a stumbling stone for those who do not believe. Could that include anybody who harbours disbelief – even believers? I think so. Following Jesus is a very varied venture. When he calls us to follow him he doesn't specify the distance. That's up to us. And, the temptation is to start measuring – especially the closer we get to him.

From a distance, everything Jesus stands for is great. How could any decent human being not be for what Jesus is for: love of God, love of neighbour, especially the weak, the exploited and those on the margins of society and even sanity? But how close to that loving do we want to get and actually do?

In his book, *God of Surprises*, Gerard W Hughes writes: 'There is a foolish prodigality, too, in the Father who is presented as leaving the ninety-nine sheep to go and hunt for the one that is lost, a foolishness which we so often correct in the church by concentrating our attention and energies on the one which is safe and leaving the ninety-nine!' (p 115)

There is no detour. That stumbling stone has us cornered. We must face it in the one who is lost, or become lost ourselves.

SIXTH SUNDAY OF EASTER

Readings: Acts 8:5-8, 14-17; 1 Peter 3:15-18; John 14:15-21

Pie in the Sky?

To an atheist – once described as someone with no invisible means of support – Christian hope must seem like a cry to on high for pie-in-the-sky. What Christians hope for, i.e. a new heaven and a new earth, has no scientific basis. Indeed it can't have. At present all that science can foresee ultimately is a frozen waste of nothingness, or a fiery finale reducing the cosmos to a compressed cinder in the Big Crunch. The heart-warming prospect of blissful eternal life has no basis other than in the word of God (Apoc 21:1).

In today's second reading Peter exhorts us to be ready always to defend that hope. And we do that basically by showing how God has kept his promises historically and by showing that his promises continue to be fulfilled today.

Historically, God promised the seemingly impossible only to fulfil it: Abraham and Sarah in advanced age beget a son, downtrodden Hebrews gain freedom from their super-power slavemasters, an eagerly awaited messiah comes, but in the most unexpected manner. Killed and seemingly defeated, he rises from death to fulfil his mission.

Today, God's promises continue to be fulfilled. He blesses us with new life, with freedom from slavery to sin, with the promise and hope of resurrection.

Yet, perhaps there is one other way to defend that hope: by allowing it put pep in our step.

SEVENTH SUNDAY OF EASTER

Readings: Acts of the Apostles 1:12-14; 1 Peter 4:13-16; John 17:1-11

Exploring the Mind of God

I was praying alone in our public church one day when three men entered talking loudly. On seeing a harmonium there, one of them told another to go bang out a few tunes on it. He tried to lift the lid. Fortunately it was locked. I just ignored them. However, when one of them declared derisively that he couldn't see God anywhere in the church, and asked the others if they could, I had to make an effort not to tell him he was looking in the wrong direction: outwards instead of inwards.

Looking inwards is not easy. It requires silence, seclusion and courage. Silence can be an endurance test when it's felt merely as an absence of noise. To work its magic, silence must come as the sound of Presence. It's the heart's reception room for God. The upper room mentioned in today's first reading, where the apostles prayed continuously, was surely that type of room. Being an upper room, i.e. above ground level, it was private and quiet – a place of retreat.

Hotels advertise weekend breaks *from* life, offering various facilities and therapies to relief stress and strain. Retreats, on the other hand, are breaks *for* life. Through the prayer, silence and seclusion they offer, the word of God can inspire and refresh us to face life anew. Retreats afford us time and space for meeting God in the silence and serenity of our heart, in the tossing and turmoil of our memories and emotions and in the hopes and plans we cherish for the future. Prayer removes the bonds that pin us to earth. Above all, it frees our imagination to explore the mind of God.

THE ASCENSION OF THE LORD

Readings: Acts 1:1-11; Ephesians 1:17-23; Matthew 18:16-20

Three Little Words

Today's gospel reading puts me in mind of a tongue-in-cheek Irish invention: an inflatable dartboard! For, if ever an author seems to score an own goal it's Matthew today. To believe in life after death is difficult enough. To believe that a specific man rose from the dead, lived among us afterwards, then ascended into heaven is gobsmacking. At least, it should be.

Therefore, you'd think that Matthew would help us to believe in Jesus' resurrection. But no! *Au contraire!* He sneaks in three little words: 'but some doubted'. Now, how could anyone – knowing that Jesus had died on a cross, yet seeing him before their very eyes – possibly doubt? What did they doubt: their own eyes, that the man before them was Jesus, that he had truly died, or what? Matthew doesn't say.

Interestingly, these doubters don't go away. Jesus commissions them too, it seems. Doubt isn't an obstacle to the mission of making disciples of all nations. And what a relief that is!

You don't have to know it all. You don't have to be rock-hard certain of everything. You can doubt and follow, perhaps even lead. Your doubting can make you seek out Jesus, until you find him.

Matthew's own-goal is actually his winning strike.

Thank you, Matthew, for those three little words.

PENTECOST SUNDAY

Readings: Acts 2:1-11; 1 Corinthians 12:3-7, 12-13; John 20:19-23

The Language of Love

I'm not one to criticise God, but I've always thought that he got it wrong with the Tower of Babel. When it comes to languages I'm hard-core pragmatic. Give me one. Any one. For all people. I abhor having to babble like a buffoon on a trip when trying to communicate in another tongue. Gesticulating with gusto and giggles is no substitute for conversation. Mutually intelligible words are vital for long-term healthy relationships. In his book, *Sing a New Song*, Timothy Radcliffe OP claims: 'Part of our deep social crisis is that we have lost confidence that words really show things as they are.'

Part of the deep spiritual crisis of the disciples, sheltering behind locked doors 'for fear of the Jews', is that the words they have been hearing don't show things as they are. Feeding on reports, rumours, and gossip about a society hostile to them doesn't really show things as they are. Just as today, feeding from a constant stream of bad news in the media gives a distorted image of society, so too with the disciples at that time. The all-important God-factor has not been pencilled in.

Then it comes. Eyes are opened, tongues are loosed, and words gush forth. Words, whose meaning is clear to all, because they flow from the one language known by all: the language of love.

THE MOST HOLY TRINITY

Readings: Exodus 34:4-6, 8-9; 2 Corinthians 13:11-13; John 3:16-18

God by any Other Name

'Trinity', a cold, abstract word is all head and no heart. Putting 'holy' before it, even 'most holy', doesn't do much for it. 'Holy' is a little on the remote side too. Listen to today's first reading and see if calling the God we meet there 'Trinity' does him justice.

Putting names on God (we have to use at least one to know whom we're talking about) does him no favours – nor us either. It can give the illusion of comprehending God to a degree that may not be true. It takes mystery from God. It seems to make him more approachable – or should that be manageable? But removing God's mystery removes his challenge.

We call God, 'Father'. We call God, 'Love'. These are the closest approximations of human language to what God is. But even these fail to do him justice. He is everything good that these words could ever imply, and much, much more besides. 'Father' and 'Love' are but tips of icebergs in a sea of mystery.

Today we celebrate God as he is: Father, Son, and Spirit. We celebrate his mystery, his unknowability. For, if God could be 'known', he would not be God. Our journey to the 'God in a cloud' of Exodus peaks when we meet the God in our heart of today. Breathtaking!

THE BODY AND BLOOD OF CHRIST

Readings: Deuteronomy 8:2-3, 14-16; 1 Corinthians 10:16-17; John 6:51-58

Shock-therapy Eucharist

Nowadays who knows, or cares, what 'manna' means? It's mentioned in today's first reading. At one level it's food provided by God for his people in the desert. Yet it's more than that. It's a lesson to drive home a fact of life: we need more than bread for survival. We need God, and every word that comes from his mouth. This is shock therapy for the Israelites, because both 'manna' and message are new, and different from what they've been used to.

Originally, 'manna' may have referred to a sweet resinous substance that exuded from a desert tree called *tamarix mannifera*. However, in John 6:49 this lowly substance prefigures the true, living bread from heaven.

That's the bread we have access to in our modern desert. Taking it, however, may be shock therapy for us too when we realise its significance. In today's gospel reading Jesus doesn't try to explain away the giving of his body and blood as food and drink. He leaves the mystery.

Whether we know, or care, what 'manna' means, we must know, and care, what Eucharist means. It means 'thanksgiving' that God is with us, among us and in us. That's the therapy. But he's also in those we hate. That's the shock.

SECOND SUNDAY IN ORDINARY TIME

Readings: Isaiah 49:3, 5-6; 1 Corinthians 1:1-3; John 1:29-34

The God Way

Charm: you have it, until you know it. It's the same with humility. Better that others be pleased with us for having it than we draw their attention to it in ourselves. If it's there, it will out – as will God's purpose in human affairs.

Take, for example, the reading: 'It is you who shall be shepherd of my people Israel, you who shall be ruler over Israel' (2 Sam 5.2). Here we have God's will for King David as ruler of his people Israel. He must act like a shepherd! Not the first model that springs to mind nowadays for civil power.

That same inscrutable intent is evident in today's gospel reading. God wants his Son to be like a lamb! How humble can you get? God really does things in strange ways. You want a ruler. You get a shepherd! Someone comes on a world-changing mission and he is to act like a lamb! Doesn't make sense. But then it's not supposed to – at least not by human reckoning.

God uses the lowly to confound the great. He always has, and always will. The ball is in our court.

THIRD SUNDAY IN ORDINARY TIME

Readings: Isaiah 8:23-9:3; 1 Corinthians 1:10-13, 17; Matthew 4:12-23

All for one?

M Scott Peck wrote in *The Different Drum*: 'Pseudo community is conflict-avoiding; true community is conflict resolving.' In today's second reading Paul would seem to hold a similar view. He appeals to the Corinthians to remember in whose name they were baptised. Respecting their common baptism in Jesus' name creates unity. As Paul asks them collectively and not individually about their baptism, they must answer collectively. They can do that only by talking constructively together first. Respect for Jesus' name is the springboard to that desired exchange.

Two things are clear here: baptism unifies; it's not automatic. Those baptised have to work with their baptism to allow it to have its effect. This doesn't mean that as soon as we recall our common baptism in Jesus' name everything is hunky dory. No more bickering, shortsighted self-interest, or breaking up into groups, gangs or factions. Call them what you will.

But what it does mean is that we'll have to do some heavy-duty thinking about why we want to be called Christian in the first place – and follow with behaviour that shows that 'why'.

Today more than ever conflict resolution, at all levels, is direly needed – today being Holocaust Memorial Day.

FOURTH SUNDAY IN ORDINARY TIME

Readings: Zephaniah 2:3, 3:12-13; 1 Corinthians 1:26-31; Matthew 5:1-12

To be or not to be?

A wit once described capitalism as the survival of the fattest. He could have said it about life in general. We prize ability above its lack. Those with skills shine brighter than those without them. They are courted, indulged and promoted. Others aren't. That's life. But not as God intended.

That's clear from today's readings: 'I will leave in the midst of you a people humble and lowly ... and no one shall make them afraid' (Zeph 3:12-13). 'God chose what is foolish in the world to shame the wise; God chose what is weak in the world to shame the strong ...' (1 Cor 1:27). What did he choose them for? Was it to do something, or to be something? The order of things here is important. God chooses people to be. Bosses choose people to do. God doesn't choose people for what they have. Bosses do. That's the difference.

When people become what God calls them to be, they then 'perform' beyond expectation. Then the 'foolish' shame the wise. Then the 'weak' shame the strong. People who think that letters after their name or titles before them make them important have a lot to learn.

And they won't learn it from books.

FIFTH SUNDAY IN ORDINARY TIME

Readings: Isaiah 58:7-10; 1 Corinthians 2:1-5; Matthew 5:13-16

A Room with no View

When the cheapest square foot of an apartment costs £6,000 and the entire apartment costs over £100 million you wonder how anyone could feel comfortable in such surroundings seeing the type of world we live in. But then the super rich who buy these apartments won't see it. What they will see is a 180-degree view of Hyde Park. Even with an address at Hyde Park, London, even with fifty-metre hallways, and 2.5 metre entrance doors, even with master bathrooms that have full height stone walls, sunken marble basins and waterproof TVs in them to boot, you instinctively feel that something is missing in all of this. That something would seem to be concern at the awful divide between the super-haves and the super have-nots.

Add to that the fact that in one year, 2010, $46.9 billion went up in smoke in the US alone – not to mention other countries – by people sucking it in, then you suspect that there's something crazily wrong in this wonderful world of ours. And all doubt goes when statistics furnished by the Food and Agriculture Organization inform us that the number of undernourished people in the world in 2010 was close to one billion.

'If you give your bread to the hungry, and relief to the oppressed,' Isaiah tells us in today's first reading, then 'your light will rise in the darkness' – even to that of a high-rise, high-value apartment with a 180-degree unrestricted view of parkland. For until the light of God's word enters there, it remains a room with no view.

The same holds true for every person estranged from God's word, no matter where they live.

SIXTH SUNDAY IN ORDINARY TIME

Readings: Sirach 15:15-20; 1 Corinthians 2:6-10; Matthew 5:17-37

Because We're Worth it!

Scientists come up with what, to the scientifically challenged, seem like strange notions. For example, Johannes Kepler (d 1630) thought that planets such as Mars and Venus could be inhabited. William Herschel (d 1822) claimed that cities nestled in craters on the moon. Closer to our day, American physicist James McDonald (d 1971) believed that UFOs had visited the earth. And, Fred Hoyle (d 2001) thought that bacteria permeated the universe and produced life on planets. And, of course, let's not forget God-delusioned Richard Dawkins who has no problem with putting his faith in the 'probability' of there being 'god-like' aliens somewhere out there.

So when the first truly earth-like planet was located in January 2011, some 560 light-years away, NASA's scientists were jubilant. Would life be found there? Alas, no! A 1,300°C temperature sears its surface and destroys its atmosphere. Radiation blasts its surface that's nearly as dense as iron. Indeed what's becoming increasingly clear is that the 500 extra-solar planets so far found feature such freaky fluctuations of roasting heat and freezing cold that finding alien life anywhere looks less likely than ever.

So when St Paul, in today's second reading, refers to a wisdom that the masters of this age – be they scientists, philosophers, politicians, journalists, or whatever – have never known, let us thank God for our privileged, even unique, position in this universe. A uniqueness that enables us to grasp in wisdom that God has prepared for those who love him things beyond the mind of man, things that no eye has seen and no ear has heard.

Created lovingly in God's image, we look forward to glory – because we're worth it.

SEVENTH SUNDAY IN ORDINARY TIME

Readings: Leviticus 19:1-2, 17-18; 1 Corinthians 3:16-23; Matthew 5:38-48

The Cheek of it!

'Would you turn the other cheek?' I ask one of the village elders as we sit at table after Mass having just listened to the same gospel reading as we hear today. It's the one that tells us to do just that: if struck on one cheek, to turn the other. I'm on one of my 'patrols', as we call them, in my parish in Flores, Indonesia. This seemingly placid septuagenarian of the friendly face instantly transmogrifies into a piece of flint with a scary scowl that leaves no doubt that neither of his cheeks would turn to an affront. He becomes animated and shoots out something in the local lingo that loosely translated goes: 'No way, José!'

Years later, back in Ireland, I ask the same question in a group and, surprise! surprise! get the same response, albeit less flinty. Turning the other cheek, regardless of who you are, or where you're from, isn't easy. Sometimes you'd think it's not even possible. But believing that would be disastrous.

Our natural state as human beings is that of peace. Violence, crime and war are aberrations – foreign bodies in our system. If someone offends us, we need to ask two questions. Is the perceived offence deliberate, or is it not? If it isn't, then there's no reason to take offence. And, if it is deliberate there's still no reason to take offence unless, that is, we want to make our antagonist happy by playing into his or her hands.

I once read that you can't hurt the feelings of a mature person. It's the neurotic and the immature one who takes offence. And that is not a cheeky comment.

EIGHTH SUNDAY IN ORDINARY TIME

Readings: Isaiah 49:14-15; 1 Corinthians 4:1-5; Matthew 6:24-34

Cost of Clutter

A report on research carried out for an insurance company in Britain reveals that the average Briton creates about 3,370 cubic feet of clutter. The space needed to contain personal possessions has doubled in 30 years. Needless to say, Britons are not unique in this matter. Most of the junk consists of clothes, books, toys, gym gizmos, electrical gadgetry, magazines and newspapers. On average 44 per cent of an individual's room is sacrificed to possessions, or junk – depending on your viewpoint – to the value of at least £2,000. Multiply that figure by population numbers and you soon come up with an astounding amount of what's little more than expensive waste. Multiply that in turn by the number of countries where such hoarding is the norm and what's astounding becomes astronomical.

So today's gospel hits the spot to clear the clutter: 'Surely life means more than food, and the body more than clothing!' In other words, we weren't born to hoard things, especially things we don't need or use. We may have been hunter-gatherers in the dim distant past, but we've evolved in the interim. Or have we? To witness the frenzied forays into stores, with sales on, makes one wonder. Can a half-priced, flat-screened TV set, or whatever the coveted item may be, be worth the discomfort and indignity of camping out all night alongside a shop front so as to be among the first to charge unbridled across the glitzy threshold of bargain land?

Better to pick some flowers and gaze in wonder on them. Savour their scent as you listen to today's gospel: 'Think of the flowers growing in the fields; not even Solomon in all his regalia was robed like one of these.'

The wisdom of God's word won't be found at sales. It's not for sale. It's always free, but never without cost.

NINTH SUNDAY IN ORDINARY TIME

Readings: Deuteronomy 11:18, 26-28, 32; Romans 3:21-25, 28; Matthew 7:21-27

A Delusion by any Other Name

In *The God Delusion* Richard Dawkins states, ' … one of the truly bad effects of religion is that it teaches us that it is a virtue to be satisfied with not understanding.' Seems there's more than one 'delusion' doing the rounds! Religion acknowledges mystery. Unlike a puzzle that can be solved, mystery is not for solving but exploring. And, by definition, it can't be sucked dry by human intelligence. It's greater than anything the human mind could ever comprehend. Otherwise it's not mystery. Any religion worth its incense delves into mystery, but with humility in the face of unknowing. It's the humility bit that's the virtue not some spurious satisfaction with ignorance.

Take today's first reading, for example: 'Today I set before you a blessing and a curse.' That's not the mystery, however. The mystery is that some people choose the curse. Now why would they do that? Don't they know the stakes? Don't they believe in curses? Don't they care one way or the other? Seems not.

Shakespeare wrote in *Hamlet* that there is nothing either good or bad but thinking makes it so. If he were writing today he might upgrade that to: 'There is nothing good or bad but DNA makes it so.' Wouldn't it be great if that were true? Just a tweak on the old DNA spiral here and a zap of the old laser beam there and hey presto: a new creation!

And if that's not a delusion, I don't know what is.

TENTH SUNDAY IN ORDINARY TIME

Readings: Hosea 6:3-6; Romans 4:18-25; Matthew 9:9-13

Keeping Low Company

About 40 years ago I read *The Two-Edged Sword* by the Jesuit biblical scholar John L. McKenzie. At this remove I can recall only one sentence from it. One that's still as sharp today as the two-edged sword he was writing about then. It still penetrates deeply, and pains. That sentence reads: 'Jesus was often accused of keeping low company. Many of his followers, however, seem to have risen above that criticism.' Ouch!

Today's gospel puts me in mind of it. 'I have come to call not the righteous but sinners.' One way of knowing that it's God's word we're hearing and not our own, is when it's difficult to take. We hear what the word is saying, but don't like it. We try to explain it away, water it down, or ignore it – but can't. It won't go away – now, or ever. It packs the same punch 40 years down the line.

When that word penetrates so does God's Spirit, directing it, planting it, nurturing it. It changes us when we trust it. Matthew trusted it as he heard Jesus call: 'Follow me.' And, it changed him. From stagnating at a tax booth he became energised to journey into the unknown.

That's another way of knowing that it's God's word we hear: it's open-ended. It can take us anywhere – especially to places we would never dream of going on our own.

ELEVENTH SUNDAY IN ORDINARY TIME

Readings: Exodus 19:2-6; Romans 5:6-11; Matthew 9:36-10:8

Lost in Translation

Today's second reading carries three terrible words, at least in the NRSV Catholic Edition. They are: 'wrath of God' (v 9). What image of God do those words conjure up: the Fuming Father, the Dour Deity, or the Spiteful Spirit? It may be just a human way of speaking about God, yet it refers to something real that we need to be saved from – or so it seems. And we need God's Son to save us from it. Are we to believe then that an angry God demands the agonising death of his Beloved Son to quench his anger? I hope not.

So what of the wrath that Paul speaks of? An interesting little footnote in the NRSV about these three woeful words tells us that the Greek has 'the wrath'. The 'of God' bit is not there. For me, that puts quite a different complexion on Rom 5:9.

The wrath now is the built-in consequence of greed, violence, corruption, and godlessness. It's humanity's self-inflicted wrath – avoidable if we but acknowledge the light of Christ and live in it. It's not the wrath of an irate God blasting mankind into oblivion. It's the disaster people bring on themselves by their godlessness.

A loving Father sent his Son into this godlessness in spite of what would happen to him, not so that it would happen. His blood justifies us; that symbol of his loving faithfulness to his Father. Only a similar faithfulness in ourselves will save us from 'the wrath'. Or, should that be 'our wrath'?

TWELFTH SUNDAY IN ORDINARY TIME

Readings: Jeremiah 12:10-13; Romans 5:12-15; Matthew 10:26-33

A Two-edged Question

Several years ago I was listening to a religious debate on radio between people of different faiths, and none. One of the participants, a Jew, asked a Christian a troublesome question. How could he (the Christian), he asked, pray to God when sick to ask for health, or worse, to be so trivial as to ask God to find something that was lost, when that God ignored the plight of 6 million Jews under Nazi tyranny.

Not an easy one that, especially in the light of today's gospel reading where Jesus tells us that even the hairs on our head are all counted (v 30). Furthermore, he assures us, that not one sparrow falls to the ground without the Father noting it. Sort of difficult to reconcile that with what happens in life at times. Isn't it?

We ask where God is when the innocent suffer, when a child dies, or is born disabled, when nature blindly kills, and people kill with open eyes, when sickness strikes, when someone takes their life. The list goes on and on.

But do we thank God when things go well, when a child is born healthy, when our luck is good, when we achieve success, when we live long and well, when we love and are loved, give and receive kindness? This list, too, could go on and on.

Our constant question to God is: 'Why do you allow evil?' Our rare question to ourselves is: 'Why do we commit it?'

THIRTEENTH SUNDAY IN ORDINARY TIME

Readings: 2 Kings 4:8-11, 14-16; Romans 6:3-4, 8-11; Matthew 10:37-42

Meditation's the Thing

Picture yourself beside a cool, mountain stream. Birds flit about and chirp softly in branches swaying slowly in a gentle breeze. You're secluded from the turbulence of that hectic place called 'the world'. The soothing cascade of a waterfall fills you with serenity. The water is crystal clear. So clear, in fact, that you can easily make out the face of the person you are holding down under water! That's one tongue-in-cheek technique for coping with stress and anger.

A more acceptable one is meditation. Recently a prominent newspaper carried, within a week of each other, two reports on meditation. One dealt with it as a therapy for depression and other mental health problems. It recommended a much wider use of it in the health service to offset over-reliance on anti-depressants.

The other report described a school-project that had 14-15-year-old students meditating for 40 minutes daily in school to cope with anxiety and stress. The project designed as an eight-week course introduces students to the benefits of silence and of developing a positive mindset.

Now if the secular world can see the benefits of meditation, how much more should we, people of faith. If we're to take seriously today's second reading we need to be concerned about what we become because of our baptism: dead to sin, alive for God. That becoming takes time and needs awareness.

English art critic and social thinker, John Ruskin (d 1900) once remarked that the highest reward for a person's toil was not what they got for it, but what they became by it. How apt indeed when applied to toiling in the vineyard of the Lord!

FOURTEENTH SUNDAY IN ORDINARY TIME

Readings: Zechariah 9:9-10; Romans 8:9, 11-13; Matthew 11:25-30

In the Arms of God

One way of knowing that it's God's word we're hearing when listening to scripture is when it disturbs us. When we try to convince ourselves that we haven't heard what we know we have. When we feel its challenge and flee it. But when it catches up with us, all doubt should go.

Today's gospel reading carries that word, guaranteed to deflate any overblown egos within hearing range. It's that bit about the Father hiding certain 'things' from the wise and the learned and revealing them to mere infants. How odd of God to choose that ruse! – to paraphrase British journalist William Norman Ewer (1885-1976).

It must be to put us in our place: the place for 'infants', for the 'little ones', the disciples of Jesus who had no learning as the scribes and Pharisees had, and who had no social standing either. The 'things' kept hidden were the signs Jesus worked as pointers to God's kingdom already present among us. Those best trained to recognise them were the very ones who couldn't. Book learning stands for zilch.

Personal effort can't propel us into the mind of God. Merely poring over the scriptures is a useless exercise. The more we pore, the more we bore. Now there's a thorny thought for biblebelters and pulpit-thumpers!

Better to be a little one in the eyes of God than a learned one in the eyes of man. Better to know your place as an infant: in the loving arms of God.

FIFTEENTH SUNDAY IN ORDINARY TIME

Readings: Isaiah 55:10-11; Romans 8:18-23; Matthew 13:1-23

One Word Only

Dionysius the Elder, tyrant of Syracuse, (430 to 367 BC) wasn't called 'the Elder' for nothing. Cunning, if not wisdom, lurked in his depths. His testy tongue once snapped, 'Let thy speech be better than silence, or be silent!' A guaranteed conversation-stopper at any party! Clearly, he wasn't into small talk.

Neither is God. Today's first reading with near-poetic elegance pictures the power of the word that emanates from God. Note the singular. One word is sufficient for God's purpose – and uttered only once. God does not repeat himself. He doesn't need dry runs. He utters his word and it goes forth, returning always but only after it fulfils its mission.

We need to hear that today. When bad things happen people still ask indignantly why God allows it. Why, in other words, doesn't he override human freedom, take back one of his greatest gifts? Why doesn't he turn the perpetrators of the bad things into robots? Hard-wire them so they wouldn't do evil? Put like that, such questions don't make much sense.

We may need convincing that despite the evil that occurs in our beautiful world, God's word is still active and potent. It operates in ways we just can't fathom. Brings results in most unexpected ways. It's a word spoken softly that breaks no silence, yet is far more powerful than silence could ever be.

It's a word we need to train to listen for – in any place, at any time, from anyone. It's a word that speaks not to the ear, but to the heart.

SIXTEENTH SUNDAY IN ORDINARY TIME

Readings: Wisdom 12:13, 16-19; Romans 8:26-27; Matthew 13:24-43

A Word for the Weeds

You can sum up today's long gospel reading in two words: Cool it! A most insightful piece of writing, it comes with a take you wouldn't expect. It puts me in mind of something the late John O'Donohue wrote in his book *Eternal Echoes* (p 89): 'Where all danger is neutralised, nothing can ever grow.' And it's growth that Jesus' parable is concerned with: your growth, my growth, and mankind's growth into the fullness of life.

Whatever harms life, is alien to it. We don't come into this world with embedded seeds of self-destruction. God creates us for life, not death; for wholeness, not sickness; for happiness, not horror; for joy, not gloom; for hope, not despair; and for glory, not damnation.

Somewhere along the line things went wrong. Still do. And when they do we shouldn't get too hot and bothered about rooting out the cause. To put it starkly, we need to be able to live with sin. Not in it, but with it. For seriously minded people of faith that is possible, but only when their God is benign. When they know him to be the Compassionate One, he who fashioned this beautiful creation so lovingly, knowing it would be marred by evil – the price to pay for freedom.

If God can live with weeds until the harvest, then so can we. So must we. They can't destroy the crop. No fear of that. But being violent with them will do more harm than good. So, cool it! God rules, not the weeds.

SEVENTEENTH SUNDAY IN ORDINARY TIME

Readings: 1 Kings 3:5, 7-12; Romans 8:28-30; Matthew 13:44-52

No Shortcuts

The *Manual of Zen Buddhism* by Cheng-tao Ke tells us that the sage:

> walks always by himself, goes about always by himself;
> Every perfect one saunters along one and the same passage of Nirvana;
> His tone is classical, his spirit is transparent, his airs are naturally elevated,
> His features are rather gaunt, his bones are firm, he pays no attention to others.

Compare that Buddhist sage to the biblical one found in today's first reading. There, Solomon prays for a discerning mind – one that can distinguish between good and evil, to enable him to govern God's people fairly. No elitism there. No focus on a lean and hungry look. Outward appearance means nothing to God. And, there's no aloofness either. No indifference to other people's plight. Quite the opposite, in fact. Biblical wisdom is geared to engagement, to service, to responsibility.

The wise one is he, or she, who knows how to live well with others. Biblical wisdom is outward looking. While it comes from on high it's found at the coalface. It's found in those who don't settle for the sidelines, who are not afraid to make the journey to authentic self. As Robert Jingen Gunn puts it in *Journeys Into Emptiness* (p 7): 'Yet we remain deeply ambivalent about becoming ourselves. Afraid of the anxiety that attends self-knowledge, afraid of the possible demands of authentic life, we run away, hiding in false selves, or smaller selves, avoiding the challenge of our true self.'

Solomon faced God, God's people and himself to acquire wisdom. There are no shortcuts.

EIGHTEENTH SUNDAY IN ORDINARY TIME

Readings: Isaiah 55:1-3; Romans 8:35, 37-39; Matthew 14:13-21

Faith's Strength

I've just finished reading *The God Delusion* by Richard Dawkins with my faith intact despite running the gauntlet of rational, and at times seemingly irrational, assault. I think that his approach to eradicating religion is rather like fighting fire with wind. It may blow it out, but then again it may just fan the flames.

Anyway, today's second reading reminds us of a very important fact with regard to faith. It's not primarily a matter of our relationship with God, but of God's relationship with us. That's its strength.

Paul puts it boldly as he asks: 'Will hardship, or distress, or persecution, or famine, or nakedness, or peril, or sword' separate us from Christ? To which he gives a resounding No! Neither will 'death, nor life, nor angels, nor rulers, nor things present, nor things to come …' (including science and Dawkins' book?) – nothing, simply nothing, can separate us from the love of God. In other words nothing can touch God's love for us. That's what we believe, wonderfully unscientific though it may be.

And the faith we have – or, more accurately, that has us – is not for hoarding but for sharing. It's a gift to improve the quality of human life by bringing out all that is good within and around us. That's the point of today's gospel reading too. The crowds are hungry, in a barren place. Jesus tells his followers – those with faith in him – to feed the crowds.

Once the faith is there, the miracle happens.

NINETEENTH SUNDAY IN ORDINARY TIME

Readings: 1 Kings 19:9, 11-13; Romans 9:1-5; Matthew 14:22-33

Shattered

In his *Hymn of the Universe* Teilhard de Chardin prays: 'Shatter, my God, through the daring of your revelation the childishly timid outlook that can conceive of nothing greater or more vital in the world than the pitiable perfection of our human organism.' (p 24) Today's first reading and the gospel put me in mind of that prayer.

They shatter the dubious certainties of small minds. They shatter the shaky security of a mind trapped inside predictable parameters, bound by the banal, fearful of the unknown, unable to probe the eternal. Those two readings come with thoughts and imagery nearly too powerful to comprehend and too incredible to accept.

You have Elijah meeting God at Horeb. And how does God appear? In a mighty rock-splitting wind? No. In a terrifying earthquake? No. In a ferocious fire? No. But in the most unlikely 'sound of sheer silence' (19:12 *NRSV*). When the clutter goes, God comes.

Then in the gospel reading you have Jesus walking on water. Another epiphany of God's presence in the creation of calm. The imagery of Psalm 107:29 is used here: 'He made the storm be still, and the waves of the seas were hushed.' When the noise and turmoil stops God's presence begins to be felt.

This is the something 'greater and more vital' that Teilhard prayed for: the realisation that God is never far away. He is active within his creation, and for a purpose. Only an outlook shattered by revelation can hope to grasp its implications.

TWENTIETH SUNDAY IN ORDINARY TIME

Readings: Isaiah 56:1, 6-7; Romans 11:13-15, 29-32; Matthew 15:21-28

Method in the Madness

It's not often that Jesus' language seems crude, but in today's gospel it does. Using the common Jewish designation for Gentiles, viz 'dogs', he says 'It is not fair to take the children's food and throw it to the dogs.' Perhaps knowing it's common coinage removes some unease at its use. Perhaps. Perhaps being so removed from the language and culture of Jesus' time the word sounds harsher now than it did then. Perhaps. Perhaps the diminutive form of 'dog' that's used, softening it to 'puppy', removes the harshness. Perhaps.

But what about Jesus' tone of voice, facial expression and body language as he utters those words? Is he surly, spiteful, or cruel? Hardly. We can all too easily picture him as almost terminally serious, without a laugh in his body. Well, if Jesus has no joy in his heart, no lightness in his spirit, no humour on his lips, then whatever else he brings it's not 'good news', and it isn't the fullness of life.

I suspect a mischievous, yet friendly, banter here between Jesus and the woman; also, that Jesus orchestrates the entire encounter to teach his disciples a lesson. She's a Canaanite, despised by Jews. Yet, she doesn't take offence in the least at what Jesus says. She even turns the tables on him and (dare one suggest it?) makes him chuckle at her wit and bowls him over by her good humour.

Clearly, that's a winning combination, for Jesus tells the 'chosen' ones that this despised one has great faith, and grants her what she wants. Nothing crude there!

TWENTY-FIRST SUNDAY IN ORDINARY TIME

Readings: Isaiah 22:19-23; Romans 11:33-36; Matthew 16:13-20

Our Inscrutable God

How do you make God laugh? Just tell him your plans! The hymn of praise that is today's second reading soaring on a loftier plane than that opening quip, nonetheless points to the same reality: the inscrutability of God.

Down from the heady heights of Paul's vision of God, what does it mean for us in daily life that God is inscrutable? Well, let's say first what it doesn't mean. It doesn't mean that we can't know anything about God, so there's no point in trying to. It means that we can't know everything about him. Coming to terms with God in our life is our number one priority, or should be. Sadly, for many it isn't.

And when we try to come to terms with God we find, as Thomas Merton points out in *Love and Living* (p 111): 'There is a disconcerting aura of secularity about much of God's activity as recorded in the Bible, and uneasiness with this has generally led certain types of philosophic religiosity to improve on the concept of God, seeking to make it more spiritual, more impressive to man's mind, in a word, more 'divine'.' Not only is that secularity found in the Bible, it's found in real life too.

Compare the number of times we're told in the Bible to pray to the number of times we're told to love our neighbour. And showing that love is very down-to-earth stuff indeed – the stuff of the Good Samaritan. The sleeves up, hands on approach.

God wants action, not just intention. There's nothing inscrutable about that.

TWENTY-SECOND SUNDAY IN ORDINARY TIME

Readings: Jeremiah 20:7-9; Romans 12:1-2; Matthew 16:21-27

God the seducer

The amazingly popular film *Into Great Silence* – the one about the Grande Chartreuse in the French Alps – has the first verse of today's first reading as a recurring refrain: 'O Lord, you have seduced me and I let myself be seduced.' It seems to be the only explanation for someone to embrace so strict a lifestyle: silent, celibate, solitary and frugal. But what a way to talk about God! And what a way for God's word to talk about God! It has an intensity to it that's almost palpable. Only someone very close to God would use such language. Only a God very close to him would allow it.

How many people get so close to God that they can speak like that about him, and to him? In those words lie a passionate history, a complex relationship and an intense hunger. Only someone with depth, passion and commitment could speak like that to God. Only someone struggling with God's approaches, doing all he can to resist them but knowing that he can't, and in his heart of hearts admitting to himself that he doesn't really want to resist them, could use such language convincingly.

Does this in any way reflect our experience of dealing with God? Do we struggle with him? Do we resist his advances? Have we felt his seduction? Have we succumbed to his will?

If it doesn't mirror our experience, if we haven't had the struggle, felt the seduction, discovered his will, then we should pray that we do. Time is short.

TWENTY-THIRD SUNDAY IN ORDINARY TIME

Readings: Ezekiel 33:7-9; Romans 13:8-10; Matthew 18:15-20

I am my Brother's Keeper

The word of God can be confusing. And thank God for that! Otherwise, we might become intolerable, especially when it comes to doing what today's first reading tells us to do: to warn the wicked when God instructs us to. The confusing bit here is how to know that we have been so instructed. As Thomas Merton once wrote in *Contemplation in a World of Action*: 'The prophetic charism is a gift of God, not a duty of man.' Becoming the moral mouthpiece for God is a tricky path to tread. That said, however, someone has to do it.

For those so called, a question to ask before giving the warning: Why does God warn the wicked? No confusion here. God wants them to change for their good, not his. Concerned, he meets them half way through his 'sentinel' (v 7).

That concern should set the tone of our warning. It should be positive not negative, gentle not harsh, life affirming not condemnatory. When approaching the wicked to convince them of the folly of their ways it's good to recall that one of the most important trips we can make in life is to meet someone halfway.

Perhaps Charles Davis should have the last word: 'Human pride has led to a notion of freedom and equality as meaning, "You're on your own." But we cannot be human on our own.' (*A Spirituality For the Vulnerable*, p 66)

TWENTY-FOURTH SUNDAY IN ORDINARY TIME

Readings: Sirach 27:30-28:7; Romans 14:7-9; Matthew 18:21-35

Bargain Basement Religion

American journalist and radio personality Franklin P. Adams, (1881-1960) once described a bargain as something you can't use at a price you can't resist. Some people approach religion as they would a bargain: pick something they don't really want but can't seem to do without.

If they would only read scripture! The word of God asks for nothing less than whole-hearted commitment: 'You shall love the Lord your God with all your heart' (Deut 6.5). We can't give just a piece of ourself to God. We can't give him our spare moments only as if he were an afterthought. We can't tell Jesus I'll follow you here but not there. We can't decide I'll love this person but not that one. I'll forgive this one but not that one. We can't, as the servant in today's gospel reading does, apply one set of values to himself and an opposing set to his brothers. We can't, in other words, have it both ways.

It's either or. We follow unconditionally, or we don't follow. If there are conditions to following Jesus, he's the one who sets them. Otherwise, he's following me, not I following him.

Today's gospel reading ends with the unforgiving servant being handed over to torturers until he pays his debt in full. The last words are those of Jesus warning that God will deal similarly with anyone who does not forgive a brother from his heart. Hard words, indeed!

A sign in a shop window reads: God help those who help themselves! I think that applies to religious bargain hunting too.

TWENTY-FIFTH SUNDAY IN ORDINARY TIME

Readings: Isaiah 55:6-9; Philippians 1:20-24, 27; Matthew 20:1-16

Whose Strange Ways?

Biologist J. B. S. Haldane once remarked that the universe is not only queerer than we might suppose, but queerer than we *can* suppose. Something similar might be said of God – though phrased more elegantly. Perhaps St Augustine's comment that 'God is younger than all else' fits the bill. Straightaway it puts us on a collision course with logic: how can he who is ever ancient, be ever new?

Not surprising then that this 'illogical' God acts in some rather strange ways. He admits so himself in today's first reading: '... my thoughts are not your thoughts, nor are your ways my ways ...' But shouldn't God be the norm, and not us? If so, then it's our ways that are strange and not his. Is it because of our strange ways of doing things that today's gospel reading seems unfair, until the denarius drops? When it does, what seems unjust to our narrow way of looking at things turns out to be incredibly generous. All the workers receive a fair wage, some a very generous one.

If this story bugs us then we have two issues, at least, to deal with: accepting God's 'right' to do as he pleases – which may not be too easy depending on how close to the bone he operates – and accepting his challenge to us to live generously. Only in facing these can we begin to see the heights where God's thoughts are found (v 9).

TWENTY-SIXTH SUNDAY IN ORDINARY TIME

Readings: Ezekiel 18:25-28; Philippians 2:1-11; Matthew 21:28-32

The Fast Line

'If my doctor told me I had only six minutes to live, I wouldn't brood. I'd type a little faster.' So said science fiction writer Isaac Asimov. Today's gospel reading put me in mind of that because it touches on an important point: the need to live authentically.

Each of the two sons in today's reading says one thing and does another. The first son, the rebellious one, who says no, represents those despised in Jewish society: tax collectors because they take money from Jews for Roman authorities, and prostitutes because they sell their services often to Roman soldiers. The second son, the yes-man, represents the religious leaders who publicly appear faithful to the Father but aren't.

Yet, when compared to the chief priests and elders – also, in fact, collaborators with the Romans to maintain the *status quo* – the despised ones fare better before God. You can't say, 'read my lips' to God. Action is what counts, action according to one's principles.

Nobody gets that action right from the word go. You have to work at it. Two steps forward, one step back is the shuffle for most of us. It's better than two steps forward in the wrong direction.

Mark Twain once wrote: 'Let us so live that when we come to die even the undertaker will be sorry.' If my doctor ever tells me I've only six minutes to live I won't brood either. I'll chuckle at that advice, hope for the best – and write a little faster. How about you?

TWENTY-SEVENTH SUNDAY IN ORDINARY TIME

Readings: Isaiah 5:1-7; Philippians 4:6-9; Matthew 21:33-43

Day for Life

When I started using a computer for the first time in 1990 I had to download some loony lingo into my brain. Acronyms were all the go. You had WYSIWYG: What You See Is What You Get, or, don't blame your computer for your silly mistakes. Another was GIGO: Garbage In, Garbage Out, or, don't blame your computer for spewing out your sow's ear instead of a silk purse.

Alive and well, the GIGO maxim applies not only to computers but also to life, especially today as we celebrate Ireland's 'Day for Life.' This celebration, an initiative of the Catholic Bishops' Conferences of Ireland, Scotland, England & Wales, is celebrated in Ireland, England & Wales and Scotland each year – in Ireland since 2001. It's a response to the proposal of the late Pope John Paul II that 'a day for life be celebrated each year in every country to foster in individual consciences, in families, in the church, and in civil society, a recognition of the meaning and value of human life at every stage and in every condition.' (*Evangelium Vitae* #85).

Now, back to GIGO, or, what you put into life is what you get out of it. In today's second reading Paul tells us what to put in: truth, honour, justice, purity, excellence, and whatever is pleasing, commendable, or worthy of praise. We should focus on these, absorbing them, savouring them and allow them to do their work of bringing happiness, gratitude, and peace into the human heart.

Perhaps, GIGO needs an update: Goodness In, Goodness Out.

TWENTY-EIGHTH SUNDAY IN ORDINARY TIME

Readings: Isaiah 25:6-10; Philippians 4.12-14, 19-20; Matthew 22:1-14

Cherry Pickers Beware!

A street-wise and disarmingly down-to-earth Christian Brother once told his class of second-year secondary students, 'The first miracle Jesus worked was to make booze!' Not a particularly reverential way of referring to the miracle of Cana. But true, nonetheless. Put that way it could be a stumbling stone for inter-faith dialogue.

You'll find more stumbling stones in today's gospel reading. Take the bit about bringing both the good and the bad to the wedding feast. Doesn't seem to matter whether you're good or bad, does it? You're invited regardless. How do you get your head around that? Let me know, if you do.

Anyway, everyone seems to be invited, and not very formally either. It's almost as if they're put on the spot in the street. Here's the invitation. Take it or leave it. It's up to you. What a godsend for freeloaders, cherry pickers and opportunists!

But wait. There is a sting in the tail. One of these, let's say a cherry picker, who 'answers the call' hasn't done his homework. Life has ground rules – and that's the most basic one of all. Poor fellow! He saunters in without a care in the world and what happens? He's out on his ear before he knows it. The reason? His dress code. Nothing to do with him being good or bad. Though come to think of it, flouting social mores can indicate arrogance, selfishness or stupidity. Flouting religious ones can indicate the same.

Whichever. Cherry pickers of the world be warned. You're on note!

TWENTY-NINTH SUNDAY IN ORDINARY TIME
MISSION SUNDAY

Readings: Isaiah 45:1, 4-6; Thessalonians 1:1-5; Matthew 28:16-20

Go and Tell!

In a youthful, uppity manner many years ago I remarked at an inter-faith dialogue meeting in Selly Oaks, Birmingham, England, that Jesus wasn't crucified because he dialogued. That remark – no less incisive for being rather obvious – didn't go down well. While useful as a getting-to-know-you exercise, thereby improving relations between different faith traditions, dialogue is not the preferred option for Christian missionary activity. It may be a necessary first step in a missionary approach, but it can hardly be considered the only, or the final one. Were Jesus sending out his disciples on mission today would he tell them to dialogue instead of to teach? Personally, I doubt it. But then I don't have a hot line to God.

Missionaries are people called to tell. They tell people basically two things: God has created them for a purpose; and, by following Jesus they fulfill that purpose most assuredly. In telling this message missionaries do more than just talk. They present truth in various ways but always with humility; they meet weakness with understanding, and they confront evil with firmness. They respect diversity; they promote growth both individually and collectively; and, they bear witness to what they say.

Put that way it doesn't really matter where you are: at home, or away, at work, or at play. If you defend truth, allow for weakness, oppose evil, respect others, promote growth, and live honestly – and do so because you love God, then you are a missionary.

What a pity that the impact of baptism is wasted on babies.

THIRTIETH SUNDAY IN ORDINARY TIME

Readings: Exodus 22:20-28; 1 Thessalonians 1:5-10; Matthew 22:3-40

Love is All You Need

The Beatles got it right: all you need is love! Trouble is, they didn't say where to get it. Neither does Jesus in today's gospel reading. A lawyer tests him with a question. Is it a genuine one to assess his depth of understanding, or a trick question to make him look foolish? It could be either. It's not the ten commandments that Jesus is quizzed about, but the Torah – with its 613 commands. Of these 248 are positive, i.e. have a 'you shall' form; 365 are negative and have a 'you shall not' form. So, just imagine being asked which of those is the greatest.

Jesus, however, remains unfazed. He ignores any deviousness on the part of the questioner. Taking the question at face value, he answers it: love God and love your neighbour. Could anything be simpler or clearer? Why then are there so many problems with human relationships and so much suffering in our world? Can loving God and our neighbour be that difficult?

Not at all! But many people prefer complexity to simplicity. Simplicity scorns wiggle room, dislikes nitpicking, finds defining and qualifying things until they're beyond recognition distasteful; and it offers no excuse for foot-dragging when action is called for.

By putting Jesus to the test, that lawyer unwittingly puts himself to the test also. Now he can never claim ignorance of what is expected of him. He has no excuse for not allowing the information he was looking for to be his guiding light.

Come to that, neither have we.

THIRTY-FIRST SUNDAY IN ORDINARY TIME

Readings: Malachi 1:14-2:2, 8-10; 1 Thessalonians 2:7-9, 13; Matthew 23:1-12

A Code of Conduct

Today's gospel reading about the Pharisees' dress code, geared to draw attention to themselves, triggers a cheeky chuckle as I recall an experience I had in Indonesia. I'm on a slow boat – not to China – to Java. Arm in a sling from a fall that had fractured my right elbow, I'm on my way for surgery in Surabaya over a thousand kilometres from where I work as a missionary. A passenger is chatting with me – a Protestant, from Timor in eastern Indonesia. He knows what a Catholic priest is so he asks only two of the usual three questions Indonesians ask on meeting foreigners: what's my name, and where do I work.

Then along comes another passenger, a friend of his, who is not Christian. Unfamiliar with celibate clerics, he asks the third question: where's my family. When I tell him I don't have one he stiffens, gives me a flinty look, turns on his heel without another word and leaves.

My priestly presence means absolutely nothing to him. What's clear is that he doesn't want anything to do with it. Since then I have come to expect that type of response from time to time. People generally don't react in that manner. But after the shocking sex-abuse scandals what priest would feel comfortable appearing in public uniformed to conform to a groomed image of presumed respectability, with not a hair out of place, cultured, refined and well-educated, with ne'er a bead of sweat nor a stray fish scale in sight – so unlike Jesus' choice of his apostles?

Jesus never required a dress code from any of his followers. What he does require is much more important: a code of conduct.

THIRTY-SECOND SUNDAY IN ORDINARY TIME

Readings: Wisdom 6:12-16; 1 Thessalonians 4:13-18; Matthew 15:1-13

Life's Poetry

Faith boldly goes where reason can't reach. It gives a breathtaking vision of life, and human destiny. It teaches that we are born to live in peace and harmony, to experience growth and maturity and to enjoy health and happiness in this life. Then it goes further and tells us that we are destined for unimaginable glory in the life to come.

Such things are not easy to talk about. Even St Paul became frustrated when he spoke in Athens. While he kept to prose, to manageable things his listeners could grasp, they listened. But when he reached the poetry, when he stepped beyond the pedestrian parameters of what they found acceptable, they laughed at him. What they found funny was Jesus' resurrection from the dead.

Hearing Paul, in today's second reading, talk again about bodily resurrection to immortality and glory may seem like the stuff of science fiction. If so, that's no reflection on faith. It just means that science fiction is catching up with some of what God's word has been saying to us for so long.

Faith presents us with some very strange things indeed, not least with God becoming man. Three little words of staggering significance. They reveal a will and a way. A will to raise us to heights we could never dream of. A way to those heights through God's self-emptying in assuming human form and accepting all the limitations that implies.

Faith goes further still. It tells us resurrection happens every time we love instead of hate, serve instead of dominate, forgive instead of punish and share instead of hoard. It puts poetry into life.

THIRTY-THIRD SUNDAY IN ORDINARY TIME

Readings: Proverbs 31:10-13, 19-20, 30-31; 1 Thessalonians 5:1-6; Matthew 25:14-30

A Talent to Bemuse

The technical support person was having difficulty identifying the problem the caller was having with her computer. After ten minutes of futile questioning he asked her the most basic question of all: 'What type of computer do you have?'

'A white one,' she replied.

You might think that a caller like that couldn't possibly have a future in computer technology. And, you'd probably be right. However, when it comes to answering God's call to do something, that sort of reckoning goes out the window. God often calls the least talented, in secular terms, to do his will. Why so? Because it must be clear that it's God's power working through the individual that gets things done, not the individual's own talents.

Look at his choice of Pope, for example. The first, I mean. An unlettered fisherman. Would we ever dream of choosing such a candidate for the post today? Definitely not. Our candidates have to be extremely well-lettered and talented, even in secular terms. Is that saying anything about our trust in God's power?

Today's gospel reading is all about trust. A man divides his property among his servants to look after it for him while he's away. What matters is not how much they earn, but how they use what he gives them. Hiding it away safely is not an option. The owner gives it for use.

We all have at least one talent. It remains a talent to bemuse until, trusting in God, we see its purpose and put it to good use.

OUR LORD JESUS CHRIST, UNIVERSAL KING

Readings: Ezekiel 34:11-12, 15-17; 1 Corinthians 15:20-26, 28; Matthew 25:31-46

That New Years's Resolution

The end is nigh – liturgically, that is, as we celebrate Our Lord Jesus Christ, Universal King. Nothing like going out on a triumphal note! However, lest we fly off in a flurry of fervour, let us listen to what that Universal King says to us today.

In the gospel reading he tells us that some of us are blessed and some are accursed. The blessed are those of us who care for the least among us, those who give food to the hungry, and drink to the thirsty; those who welcome the stranger and clothe the naked; those who care for the sick and visit prisoners. The accursed are those of us who do none of this. Now that is not what you'd expect to hear a universal king say. In fact you wouldn't expect him even to be aware of the lowly and the least.

But therein lies the greatness of his kingdom: his concern for the weakest. When we pray The Lord's Prayer we say, 'may your kingdom come'. We want God's kingdom to establish itself universally as soon as possible. I wonder do we realise that we have a say in that happening. Though the time for its glorious coming is set and known by the Father alone, his determining of that time just may be influenced by the quality of care that we give to the weakest among us.

No need to wait for 1 January to make a New Year's resolution to give that care.

FIRST SUNDAY OF ADVENT

Readings: Isaiah 63:16-17, 64:1, 3-8; 1 Corinthians 1:3-9; Mark 13:33-37

Present Perfect

We need Advent to teach us patience. It can teach us more than that, of course. However, with our busy lifestyles we need to relearn how to be patient with, rather than how to put up with, something or someone. That busyness results in us wishing our life away. We become edgy and tense with the present and slide easily into the future – be it only into the hour ahead of us. We develop the 'when I …' mentality: when-I-get-home, when the weekend arrives, when the summer is here, when I get my new car, when I … when I … when I. The future seems to hold the carrot, the present the stick. And as we lose touch with the present, we lose touch with ourselves.

And how easy that is. During the summer I saw a pub advertising a fancy dress Christmas bash for the middle of July. For many years now venues for Christmas parties have to be booked months in advance. And it's no surprise anymore to hear and see promotions for summer holiday deals the day after Christmas. We are being programmed to live in the future as if the present doesn't count. More and more of life's rhythms are set by the world of commerce than by the world of nature.

Advent slows us down. It alerts us to prepare for Christmas, not to start celebrating it. Our gospel reading today alerts us to something else: the Lord's return. That alertness is for now, for we can meet the Lord at any time.

SECOND SUNDAY OF ADVENT

Readings: Isaiah 40:1-5, 9-11; 2 Peter 3:8-14; Mark 1:1-8

Pulling a Fast One

Today's second reading reminds me of the tale of Ted. Ted thought he'd pull a fast one on God. So he prayed: 'Heavenly Father, for you a million years is but a minute and a million Euro but one cent. Please hear me as I ask you for just one cent.' God heard, and said: 'Sure, Ted. Just a minute!'

The moral of the story is that we should know what to expect from God. Our first reading tells us what that is: tenderness. Let that sink in. God gives us his affection. Since it's not possible for us to be on a par with God, God puts himself on a par with us: he becomes man.

That's the God who comes at Christmas. But do we want to meet him? Can we tolerate a tender God? If we stamp others as our 'enemy', can we hear God's tender voice – especially when it's directed at those 'enemies'? If my enemy's enemy is indeed my friend, is his friend then my enemy? How can we call God 'friend' while calling his friend 'enemy'?

Advent is a time for thinking things through; for seeing the implications of Jesus' birth. He came to give life in all its fullness to humanity in all its numbers regardless of who they are or where they come from. That's a message you won't see posted in shop windows in the run-up to Christmas. You won't hear it shouted from housetops. You won't hear it anywhere except in God's subversive, yet creative word.

THIRD SUNDAY OF ADVENT

Readings: Isaiah 61:1-2, 10-11; 1 Thessalonians 5:16-24; John 1:6-8, 19-28

A Voice in the Wilderness

Recently I contacted a company on behalf of my province. This company could register me only as 'Mr', 'Mrs', or 'Ms'. 'Fr' or 'Rev' was not a programmed option. I settled for 'Mr'. Then the members of my Order, on whose behalf I had approached the company, could enter the company's computer only as 'employees'. It was not programmed to recognise 'religious' as a legitimate species.

Since then I've developed a new empathy with John the Baptist who, in today's gospel reading, describes himself as 'the voice of one crying out in the wilderness'. In moments of disappointment, or gloom that come – and mercifully go – it seems to me that society at large is that wilderness. You wonder who's listening to you, whether you're preaching in public, or being published in periodicals. But it's not listening to me that's the concern, or indeed listening to anybody else, for that matter. The concern is people's level of attention to the word of God.

The vociferous ones who came to John the Baptist came to confront him, not to listen to him. Sent by those who pulled the strings, i.e. the Pharisees, they demanded that he give an account of himself. As followers of Jesus, we too must give an account of ourselves for we make some extraordinary claims; not least that the Creator of all that is would want to be born a human being, and could do no better than start life in a manger!

Who in their right mind would want to listen to that?

FOURTH SUNDAY OF ADVENT

Readings: 2 Samuel 7:1-5, 8-12, 14, 16; Romans 16:25-17; Luke 1:26-38

Turn of the Knob

If the first sign of maturity is discovering that the volume knob also turns to the left, perhaps the first sign of spiritual maturity is discovering that God knows how to turn the knob. Today's first reading says as much when God tells Nathan to say to David: 'Are you the one to build me a house to live in?' In other words: 'Do you think that I need you?'

We can forget that God rules, not us. Our second reading shows God at work within human history as it talks of the mystery kept hidden for long ages but now disclosed. God creates the mystery, keeps it a mystery, and in his own good time reveals it. Our emptiness may be God's purpose being fulfilled – though not as we expect it. What seems like inactivity, or indifference, on God's part in the face of human tribulation may be his wisdom at work waiting for the opportune time to act – a time constrained by human freedom and its consequences. We need humility to admit that we don't know it all and can be wrong in our judgements. And we need trust to accept that God is never wrong in his.

He wasn't wrong in choosing a manger instead of a throne, in choosing faithfulness to his mission over personal safety, in accepting death on a cross rather than public acclaim based on false hopes. He wasn't wrong because these ended in resurrection and glory. But no one could see it at the time.

This Advent, can we?

THE FEAST OF THE IMMACULATE CONCEPTION

Readings: Genesis 3:9-15, 20: Ephesians 1:3-6, 11-12; Luke 1:26-38

A Taste for Innocence

We must never lose our taste for innocence – especially our own. How many adults can claim to still have theirs? Alas, how many think that losing innocence is inevitable, even essential to the process of growing up?

On this feast of the Immaculate Conception of the Blessed Virgin Mary we celebrate innocence. We go on record that we believe it's possible, desirable and necessary to possess a goodness that's pure, real, empowering and adult.

The Creator's high regard for innocence shines through today's first reading. Innocence in Eden was Adam and Eve's natural, unselfconscious harmony with God and with each other. They didn't need to hide themselves from God or cover themselves before each other until the serpent violated their innocence. That's the shameful thing it did. You can feel its corrosive malice as you lament the permanent damage it did to human beings. The same holds true today for anyone who violates another's innocence. You can feel a heavy sadness soak into your bones when you think of what people do to each other at times.

So, on this feast may we renew our appreciation for innocence. It was complete harmony with Mary, on God's part, even from before her birth that confers on her the title 'Immaculate Conception'. It was her innocence, her harmony with God that enabled her to take on the very adult responsibility of bringing God into this world.

We too bring God to others through our innocence – through our harmony with him – especially to those who have lost theirs.

THE MASS OF CHRISTMAS DAY

Readings: Isaiah 52:7-10; Hebrews 1:1-6; John 1:1-18

God's Christmas Face

Instead of facing the baby in the crib as a human being this Christmas, try to face him as the incomprehensible Being that he is: God. Just three squiggles of ink on paper, 'God' is a term that symbolises the mother of all being, if you'll pardon the expression. It's a sign and a sound that links us to that Being yet reveals nothing of him. To relate to him personally we need to see a human face. And what easier face to relate to than that of a baby? No challenge there.

But listen to our second reading: 'He (the Son, once the baby Jesus) is the reflection of God's glory and the exact imprint of God's very being, and he sustains all things by his powerful word.' Then go back to the first reading of Advent's first week: 'O that you would tear open the heavens and come down, so that the mountains would quake at your presence' (Is 64:1). No sweet baby's face there. Now the challenge: how to relate to that awesome God?

We need to sense God's power and majesty, and his utter strangeness, to feel the gobsmacking wonder of the Baby's birth. We can't comprehend a being without a beginning. It's so far off our mental radar that we rarely think about it. But how can we mature spiritually if we don't? So let's test our feelings towards him who can tear open the heavens and make the mountains quake – and then look in utter disbelief at the child smiling at us from the crib?

THE HOLY FAMILY

Readings: Genesis 15:1-6, 21:1-3; Hebrews 18:11-12, 17-19; Luke 2:22-40

Family Fortunes

The word of God doesn't deal in half measures, even when telling a story. Take today's first reading, from Genesis. Abraham, incredibly, becomes a father at the overripe age of 100. And Sarah, advanced in years and barren all her life, gives birth to a child. The message is clear and challenging: nothing is impossible with God.

What's also clear is that God's gift of life blossoms in spite of all threats to it. In Isaac's case, parents so old they could die while he is still an infant. What would happen then? But God is not stupid, confused, or whimsical. Nobody and no thing can thwart his plan. Even when it seems – incomprehensibly – that God wants Isaac dead you know that there's something else at stake. That's the conviction that you can't go wrong by being faithful to God's will, even when it seems to make no sense.

Did it make sense for Jesus to be conceived out of wedlock? Not a good start to life. Did tongues wag? Did it make sense for Jesus to be crucified as a despised criminal? Not a good end to life. Did fingers point? Yet God was fulfilling his plan in spite of it – and continues to do so today.

Today's feast has an important message for all families, but especially those experiencing difficulties. Wagging tongues, pointing fingers, and apparent failure in life mean nothing to God. What count are: integrity, faith in his promise, the courage to take him at his word and act upon it in full measure.

SECOND SUNDAY AFTER CHRISTMAS

Readings: Sirach 24:1-2, 8-12; Ephesians 1:3-6, 15-18; John 1:1-18

Not All in the Mind

Dreams are mysterious. Modern research into these mirages of the mind can still only dream of discovering their significance and explaining why we have them at all. However, what is clear is the close link between dreams and memories. Studies show that while we dream, our brain's temporal lobe – that facilitates memory – is fully active. If we recall our dreams we'll see that their contents reflect our experiences and our memories of them. Dream activity seems to be the brain's attempt to integrate and organise memories. Of interest too is the view of some researchers that dreams could be of use to interpret the future. This conclusion is based on studies of amnesiacs who, without their memories, to all intents and purposes have no future.

Thankfully, that's not a conclusion we would draw from today's second reading. There our future is assured because it's based not on memory of the past but on faith in God's action. For we're told that God the Father had chosen us to become his adopted children through Jesus Christ, not only before our birth but even before the birth of the world.

Only God could be so certain about the future. And if he can be, surely then, so can we. There's no place for pessimism in God's plan for us because God is in charge, not us. Paul prays that God may enlighten the eyes of our mind so that we can see the hope his call holds for us.

While that's something to dream about, it's not a dream that's linked to memory. It's a vision that's founded on hope.

THE EPIPHANY OF THE LORD

Readings: Isaiah 60:1-6; Ephesians 3:2-3, 5-6; Matthew 2:1-12

Epiphany Now

In his book, *Celibacy: A Way of Loving, Living and Serving,* Richard Sipe writes: 'Only those who see the invisible can do the impossible.' (p 168) Today's feast, The Epiphany of the Lord, is about catching a glimpse of the invisible. We're celebrating three sightings of The Lord of the Universe in the person of Jesus of Nazareth: in the baby the Magi pay homage to, in the one over whom the heavens open at baptism and in the wonder worker who turns water into wine at Cana.

But, we're celebrating present-day sightings too. For example, when we gaze on those we love: wife, husband, son, or daughter what do we see? Just a skin-covered form? Does not something deeper than skin tug at your heart and bring out the best in you? Don't we sense we're in the presence of something we can't name? That in the one we love and know intimately there's a space we've never entered and never will? When the mystery of another person touches us, we make a sighting. An epiphany happens and we're never the same again. We're the better for it. Their beauty touches us powerfully, and we know we're in the presence of something mysterious, wonderful and even sacred. Their beauty, reflecting the image and likeness of Another, opens on to eternity giving us a glimpse of what lies beyond.

Epiphany Now is what we celebrate: the cosmic Christ bursting through the earthly Jesus; and the divine light shining through those we love – and on a clear day even shining through those we don't.

THE BAPTISM OF THE LORD

Readings: Isaiah 55:1-11; 1 John 5:1-9; Mark 1:7-11

No Empty Word

As a missionary in Indonesia I baptised hundreds of babies, but only one adult. Part of a Holy Saturday vigil, that adult baptism hugely impressed the congregation by the dignity of its rite and the sincerity of its candidate. Seeing an adult freely and joyfully commit himself to Jesus for life in public was a compelling sign of God's Spirit at work.

Today's feast, the Baptism of the Lord, is a reminder of our own baptism. For those of us baptised as babies it's a non-event because we can't remember it. Its impact is not what it might have been had we been adult when baptised. However, we have ratified what our parents did on our behalf either negatively by not discarding our faith, or positively by making a conscious decision at some stage of our life to continue being a follower of Jesus. Either way, today's reading is Is 55:1-11 where God says that his word does not return to him empty but fulfils its mission, and Mk 1:7-11 where God calls Jesus his beloved son in whom he is well pleased, applies to us baptised.

In baptism God gives us a mission. It's a mission to make him known to our world, especially to those who do not know him. While that mission is general to all baptised, the way we carry it out is specific to ourselves. Realising we have it, and discovering how to carry it out gives purpose to our life – and makes us the beloved son, or daughter, in whom the Father is well pleased.

FIRST SUNDAY OF LENT

Readings: Genesis 9:8-15; 1 Peter 3:18-22; Mark 1:12-15

Reading in the Wilderness

I've heard it said that some people who suffer from burnout have never been on fire. Ouch! Today's gospel reading brings that to mind: 'And the Spirit immediately drove him out into the wilderness.' No sooner does the Father declare Jesus to be his Son, the Beloved, than the Spirit shunts him off to the wilderness. Why? So that the ecstasy of his baptism doesn't turn his head? So that his divinity doesn't overpower his humanity? So that he opts for service and not for privilege? Fired with the Spirit he hurries there to learn how to read his person and his mission.

A plan of cosmic scale clicks into play. The air tingles with urgency as Jesus reaches the wilderness. The words of Paul (Rom 8. 22-23) time travel back to us, 'We know that the whole creation has been groaning in labour pains until now … and we ourselves groan inwardly while we wait for adoption, the redemption of our bodies'. That's what the urgency is about: humanity's impending redemption.

It's what we groan for to fill the emptiness within us. It's what we search for to complete ourselves as a person. But have we learnt how to read our person and our mission? If we've not allowed God's Spirit to fire us to seek the wilderness, we will groan for all the wrong things: money, power, fame, drugs and sex – and just burn out.

Lent leads us into the wilderness. Let us enter and spend time there with the demons and the angels.

SECOND SUNDAY OF LENT

Readings: Genesis 22:1-2, 9-13, 15-18; Romans 8:31-34; Mark 9:2-10

The Story's the Thing

If there's one thing you shouldn't do after listening to today's first reading from Genesis it's to ask, 'How could God possibly want Abraham to murder his son?' He didn't.

It's a story. It carries the word of God that tells us some important truths. First, God doesn't make mistakes in those he picks for special missions. Second, God's plan for his creation cannot be thwarted even when the odds seem stacked against it. Third, freedom is not to be feared but welcomed when seasoned by loving faithfulness to God's will. Fourth, Abraham – and other people too – can be genuinely high-minded, honestly self-sacrificing and totally obedient to God. This, in sharp contrast to what the media and the entertainment industry often throw at us as they portray humans as violent, brutish, out of control.

What more effective way to convey those good things than by story telling! Journalists didn't write scripture. Those who did were both creative and inspired. We'll miss that if we allow the sizzle to steal the steak. The sizzle is Abraham's knife poised to plunge into his son's young heart at God's command. The steak is the message that God knows what he's doing. He's not whimsical. He's totally in command, and his commands are always for the good.

We, moderns, need such ancient stories to capture our imagination, and inspire our spirit. God's word is creative in its approach to us. Let our response to it be creative too. Let us turn the prose of our daily plodding into the poetry of faith-filled flight.

THIRD SUNDAY OF LENT

Readings: Exodus 20:1-7; 1 Corinthians 1:22-25; John 2:13-25

Christ Crucified

Paul preaches 'Christ Crucified' in today's second reading, not the crucifixion. There's a huge difference between the two. The one focuses on Christ; the other on suffering. While the gospels describe his suffering and death, they don't dramatise them with lengthy and graphic descriptions of flowing blood and torn flesh. There's an important lesson to be learnt in the gospel accounts of Jesus suffering and death that focusing on pain and ripped flesh won't provide.

Put simply the lesson is: it was not Jesus' suffering that was the primary part of God's salvific plan, or even primary to our redemption. No! It was the spirit that enabled him to suffer come what may. That spirit was his loving faithfulness to his Father's will. It was this love in Jesus' heart that effected our redemption, not his suffering, which would have had no value had it not been endured because of love. This view may be unacceptable to those of a certain type of spirituality. However, nothing should get in the way of that understanding – especially not a penance-promoting spirituality that makes a 'no-pain-no-gain' claim where God is concerned.

For if suffering was the non-negotiable part of God's plan, what sort of an image does that present of him? A Father, who would want his beloved son in whom he was well pleased to suffer cruelly and be killed – and all to gratify his anger at human sinfulness!

That would certainly be a stumbling block, I'd say – and to more than the Jews.

FOURTH SUNDAY OF LENT

Readings: 2 Chronicles 36:14-16, 19-23; Ephesians 2:4-10; John 3:14-21

Our Twilight Zones

In his book, *Sophie's World,* author Jostein Gaarder writes, 'The most subversive people are those who ask questions. Giving answers is not nearly as threatening. Any one question can be more explosive than a thousand answers.' Why so?

Perhaps a quote from another author may provide a partial answer. In *Kissing the Dark,* Mark Patrick Hederman writes, 'Fixation upon any one particular aspect of the total mystery is missing the point, is swapping the glory for the gore, trading our birthright for a mess of pottage. The crucifixion is not a fact. It cannot be nailed down to one explanation, labelled with one easy heading. It is an event.' Today's gospel reading tells us that some people don't just prefer the darkness, they love it. They are the ones fixated on the gore, not the glory.

John makes no excuses for these people. There is no attempt to explain away their evil deeds or mitigate their guilt. It's either or. Either you're for the light, or for the dark. Faith has no twilight zones.

Lent is a time for discovery; for facing fact not fiction, for honesty about twilight zones we may frequent, or long to: haunts of unreality, dead end traps that stunt our growth, imprison us in addiction, alienate us from each other and from God. Lent is a time for lingering in the light, for letting its rays do their healthy work. It's a time for asking the subversive question: Where does my heart lie, in darkness or in light?

FIFTH SUNDAY OF LENT

Readings: Jeremiah 31:31-34; Hebrews 5:7-9; John 12:20-30

As You Like it

Usually I pick the bits of scripture that I like. But not now. Verse 8 in today's second reading grabs my attention and won't let go. The reason? It makes no sense: Jesus learning obedience through suffering! Does that mean that had he not suffered he would have been disobedient? If so, to whom? His Father? Unthinkable!

So, what is the author saying? Thank God for academics! Even though Richard Rohr in *Things Hidden* writes, 'In fact none of the Bible appears to be written out of or for academic settings' nevertheless thanks to someone's academic study of scripture a person like me can discover that in Greek there's a play on words here. The Greek for 'learned' is *emathen,* while the Greek for 'suffered' is *epathen*. The purpose of this wordplay may be to convey the close relationship between faithfulness to God and ability to face the suffering that results from such faithfulness in a sinful world.

So instead of verse 8 being a conundrum, pessimistic and negative in tone, it's now a positive and upbeat statement. It tells us that obedience (better still 'faithfulness') to God's will and suffering go hand-in-hand to some degree. But most important of all: the suffering doesn't harm the faithfulness. It can even perfect it. Furthermore, it tells us that faithfulness to God permeates all of life. Faith does not dwell in compartments, but apartments. There are no God-free zones. Facing God means facing life with all its joys and sorrows.

Perhaps I should pay more attention to the bits I don't like.

PALM SUNDAY

Readings: Isaiah 50:4-7; Philippians 2:6-11; Mark 14:1-15:47

Fast-forwarding Pain

Why fast-forward Jesus' suffering and death to Palm Sunday? Why can't we wait for Good Friday? Today's celebration is joyous, even triumphal. Why spoil it by anticipating Jesus' suffering and death? Strange that Christianity, a religion of joy, can't celebrate today's joyous event without insisting on a long reading of Jesus' suffering and death in today's gospel reading.

Today's first reading says, 'the Lord has opened my ear' – and I hear a question: Why not allow Jesus his moment of glory, and us our moment of joy? For a moment only it is. The triumph doesn't last long. We know that. Time enough to focus on suffering when Good Friday comes. Then it would have even greater impact as we moved from the exuberance of Palm Sunday and the coziness of Holy Thursday to the horror of Good Friday, then soar to the elation of Easter Sunday.

Too quickly focusing on suffering, perhaps thinking it God-willed, presents a false image of God. Anyone inclined to do so should recall God's words to the prophet Ezekiel, 'Say to them, "As I live," says the Lord God, "I have no pleasure in the death of the wicked but that the wicked turn from their ways and live ..."' (Ezek 33:11) Neither does he take pleasure in the sinner's suffering. And most definitely, not in his Son's.

It's important that we be people of joy, even when faced with suffering. Let us celebrate joy exclusively when the occasion merits it. Palm Sunday is one such occasion.

EASTER SUNDAY

Readings: Acts 10:34, 37-43; Colossians 3:1-4; John 20:1-9

Not Seeing is Believing

Is seeing really believing? Well, in the case of the 'other disciple' in today's gospel reading it's what he doesn't see that convinces him: Jesus' corpse. He doesn't see the resurrection. What he does see is the results of it in his new depth of faith in Jesus as the Risen Christ, and later in the formation of Christian communities that the resurrection brings about.

This is the two-edged sword of God's word at work – one edge being the positive, and the other the negative. The seeing, and the not seeing. Seeing something new in ourselves, or in others, which wasn't there before, or at least not in the same way, or to the same degree; something that indicates growth, that points to the Spirit at work within us.

The Spirit that transformed Jesus of Nazareth to the Risen Christ is the same Spirit at work within us individually and collectively. It's the Spirit that gives new life. When we open ourselves to that Spirit's influence we too are transformed. Gone is the old self with its pride and selfishness, with its anger and resentment, with its backbiting and constant criticising, and with its jealousies and lusts.

Let us hurry to peek inside the sepulchre of our old self and surprise ourselves by what we do not see there. Then let us fall on our knees in gratitude to God for what he has done, in spite of ourselves.

Jesus lives! We are living proof of that – often more than we realise, or dare hope to be.

SECOND SUNDAY OF EASTER

Readings: Acts 4:32-35; 1 John 5:1-6; John 20:19-31

Locked doors

I don't know if you're into symbolism, but try this for size: locked doors that mean nothing to the resurrected Jesus. Signifying security to the disciples, they are of no hindrance whatsoever to the power of Jesus' resurrection entering that sealed room in today's gospel reading, or to that same power going out.

John doesn't describe Jesus as walking through the doors. No Hollywood special effects here. He states simply that Jesus 'came and stood among them'. Such simplicity conveys clearly just how insignificant locked doors are.

So how about our 'locked doors'? God's word is telling us that his power can be with us even though we are locked into ourselves. We don't have to open them first for God to enter!

Just think of that and what it implies! We can burden ourselves with all sorts of baggage on our journey through life. We can lock out people and events from our mind and heart to preserve our sanity or our comfort. We can circle the wagons and live in fear of life's threats and dangers. We can run from life and its challenges. Our locked doors can be all sorts of things: prejudices, fears, neuroses, selfishness, anger, whatever. Now this is the important bit of the symbolism. We don't have to unlock those doors for God to come and stand with us. In fact, we wouldn't be able to.

Mission doesn't demand perfection. The disciples got their mission behind locked doors. So do we: to proclaim that God stands among us.

THIRD SUNDAY OF EASTER

Readings: Acts 3:13-15, 17-19; 1 John 2:1-5; Luke 24:35-48

In the Wounds

In *A Risen Christ in Eastertime,* Raymond E. Brown writes: 'Today disbelief flows from many factors including unconvincing signs, e.g. the proclamation of Christ by some who scarcely resemble him.' Resembling Christ means having wounds and showing them. Not something most of us would want to have, or wish to do.

You'd think that the Risen Christ would use something else to dispel the doubts of the disciples in today's gospel reading. He uses the breaking of bread to open the minds of two disciples travelling to Emmaus. Now he uses his wounds to quell the doubts of others. Even his startling and sudden appearance among them isn't enough to rid them of doubt. But in his wounds they recognise him. Needless to say, these aren't any old wounds.

They are the wounds the world inflicts on those who love God above all else. They are the wounds of those who proclaim God's truth even when it threatens powerful vested interests. They are the wounds of those who live for others more than for themselves. They are the wounds of those who don't count cost. They are wounds that once accepted are healed and become a source of health for others. We carry them with us in life, but they carry us into eternity.

Resembling Jesus means facing the foe within our own gilded Gethsemanes; forgiving the tormentors who crucify us daily on our petty Golgothas; defeating the demons of our imaginings in the wilderness of our making; and in the longings of a lonely heart in prayer before God.

FOURTH SUNDAY OF EASTER

Readings: Acts 4:8-12; 1 John 3:1-2; John 10:11-18

All-enfolding

Today's gospel reading has Jesus saying something rather intriguing: 'I have other sheep that do not belong to this fold. I must bring them also, and they will listen to my voice. So there will be one flock, one shepherd.' Two things here are surprising.

First, Jesus claims ownership over other 'sheep' without saying who they are, or whether they know they are his. Are these Jews, or Gentiles? Is this claim valid today? If it is, whom does it include: those of other religions, those of none?

Second, the sequence of events is surprising: 'I must bring them also, and they will listen to my voice' (when I do so?). You would expect that they listen first, and then follow. But no! Jesus leads; the listening follows.

How should we view the church's mission in the light of this understanding of what Jesus says? Well, it means that wherever mission goes, God is there already. There is no such thing as a 'God-less' people, or a 'God-forsaken' place. We have to acknowledge that in God's sight, if not in ours, 'others' are in the fold. They may not know this, but we should. Consequently, basic to mission is the task of making people aware of Jesus bringing them into the fold.

Then follows mission's second task: enabling those in the fold, newcomers and those of long-standing alike, to listen to Jesus' voice through hearing his word. Consequently, familiarity with his word on the part of those on mission is essential. Otherwise, whose voice will they be listening to?

FIFTH SUNDAY OF EASTER

Readings: Acts 9:26-31; 1 John 3:18-24: John 15:1-8

Comfort in the Spirit

In his book *Things Hidden* Richard Rohr writes: 'Isn't it ironic that most of the gospel has probably been preached and taught by people who are very comfortable? That's almost an assurance that these preachers will largely miss the point, that they will not preach the true or full message' (p 104). This comes to mind on hearing today's first reading. Referring to the early church Luke writes: 'Living in the fear of the Lord and in the comfort of the Holy Spirit, it increased in numbers.'

According to Rohr, it seems, comfort and blindness to truth go hand-in-hand. Are we then to hold discomfort, insecurity, and borderline poverty as kingdom values – ones we need to live by to be members of the kingdom of God? That would be a tall order for many if so. While Jesus doesn't appear in the gospels as 'very comfortable,' neither does he appear destitute.

Jesus' 'discomfort' comes from opposing hypocrisy wherever he finds it. Taking a stance against hypocrisy threatens his safety and forces him to the margins of society – even to the most extreme of margins: Golgotha.

There may be a time for that, although we pray, lead us not into temptation – do not put us to the test. But there is a time for enjoying the 'comfort of the Holy Spirit', for enjoying the warm and healthy glow that goodness, sincere service, and holiness of life can produce. Indeed, we are called to be comfortable people; but comfortable with God's Spirit, not with the hypocrisy around or within us.

SIXTH SUNDAY OF EASTER

Readings: Acts 10:25-26, 34-35, 44-48; 1 John 4:7-10; John 15:9-17

Appeasing God

Today's second reading is a tricky one. Having just told us the wonderful news that 'God is love' John now seems to undo it all by saying that God 'sent his Son to be the atoning sacrifice for our sins'. Here we have that seemingly awful image of God, as he who demands appeasement for the sins of humanity by the death of his beloved Son. So which is it? It can't be both, can it? How can a God who is love possibly want the one he loves to be slaughtered to appease him? To put it bluntly: is there some way of honouring the text without dishonouring God?

Now you can try to resolve the dilemma by saying it is God's love for us that compels him to send his son to be killed. But, the possibility that God could love human beings more than his 'beloved' son stretches the mind that little bit too far, don't you think? If God, indeed, is love, and totally independent in how he expresses it, then why on earth would he demand sacrificial appeasement? Does that not smack of hardness of heart, even vindictiveness?

You may introduce justice into the equation and claim that divine justice demands it. But is that not making love subservient to justice? And love is greater. Indeed, as Paul says in 1 Cor 13:13, 'the greatest of all is love'. Once God forgives, justice goes out the door.

So, are love and demands for appeasement mutually exclusive? If you find out, let me know.

SEVENTH SUNDAY OF EASTER

Readings: Acts of the Apostles 1:15-17, 20-26; 1 John 4:11-16; John 17:11-19

Diamonds or Pearls?

In 2009 a buyer parted with €2.05 million for a rare 2.52 carat green diamond ring, Sotheby's revealed. The priciest sparkler of its kind ever, it was nearly enough to make the common-garden variety turn green with envy. Also a ruby and diamond necklace and earrings made in 1884 for the Duchess of Roxburghe sold at auction for €3.86 million – five times the expected price.

People pay astronomical amounts of money for things they can see, touch and possess. But how about things of much greater and more enduring value that they can't see? Things mentioned in today's second and third readings, for example: faith, hope and love. But then no amount of money can buy these. Their value is seen not at auction but in action. It's only when we give clear witness to these values that they truly sparkle. And they enhance our person like no jewellery on earth could ever do.

Another difference between these priceless values for the marketplace and the pricey baubles for auctions is that they are not for hoarding but for sharing. The more people who have them, the richer life becomes. No one would ever think of stealing them. We need never lock them up. They adorn us day and night for all to see.

Their sparkle should not blind anyone to what they reveal: the presence of God within. As John says in the second reading: 'No one has ever seen God; but as long as we love one another God will live in us.'

That pearl of great price beats hands down for value any diamond of any carat or any colour.

THE ASCENSION OF THE LORD

Readings: Acts 1:1-11; Ephesians 4:1-13; Mark 16:15-20

Strange Attractor

In his book, *Jesus Today,* Albert Nolan writes, 'It seems that systems of various kinds often exist in a state of chaos or, as they say, "on the edge of chaos," and then suddenly and unpredictably there emerges something called a "strange attractor" that rearranges the chaos into some new order.' Today, on the feast of the Ascension we celebrate not the arrival but the departure of the strange attractor: the Risen Lord.

Change 'systems' to 'individuals' above and you have many a person's life's story. Confusion and doubt are necessary for intellectual and psychological growth. As Timothy Ferris writes in *Coming of Age in the Milky Way,* 'Yet it is turmoil and confusion and not calm assurance that mark the growth of the mind.'

Into our personal confusion steps the 'strange attractor'. As we flounder, his helping hand pulls us up and out of our confusion – not, however, on to a placid and permanent plateau, but to a higher level of confusion. No sooner are our feet placed firmly on Mother Earth than we are whisked to heights that make us dizzy. If our faith doesn't s-t-r-e-t-c-h our mind, we're not people of faith, but people of reason.

Belief in the Ascension should make us gasp. Do we realise what we're saying we actually believe in! First: that someone flatline dead didn't just revive and return to his former state but resurrected to a higher, super-human, everlasting one. Second: having done so, then 'ascended' to a totally new quantum-leap environment we call 'heaven'.

Wow! Wow! And wow again! is all I can say.

PENTECOST SUNDAY

Readings: Acts 2:1-11; Galatians 5:16-25: John 15:26-27, 16:12-15

Taxi driver

This story tells what Pentecost is about. A taxi driver arrives at an address. He honks his horn. No response. He honks again. Still no response. Out he gets and knocks on the door. A stressed voice cries out, 'Just a minute, please.'

After a long pause he hears something being dragged to the door. A frail old woman in her 80s opens the door pulling a suitcase after her. 'Would you carry my case to the car, please?' she asks. 'Sure,' he says, and as he moves off she links his free arm and walks slowly with him to the taxi.

She gives him an address and asks him to go through the city centre. 'It's not the shortest way, Mam,' he says to her. 'I don't mind,' she replies, 'I'm going to a hospice. There's no hurry.'

He looks in the rear-view mirror, and sees tears in her eyes as she reveals, 'I've no family left. The doctor says I haven't long to go.' As she says that the driver leans over and quietly switches off the metre.

They drive around the city centre. She points out where she had worked in an insurance office, where she and her husband had lived after their wedding, and a building that once was a ballroom where she had first met him. At one or two places they stop in silence – her mind elsewhere. Much later they reach the hospice.

The taxi driver goes home lost in thought, convinced and content that he has just had one of the most important days of his life.

Pentecost means using the language of love.

THE MOST HOLY TRINITY

Readings: Deuteronomy 4:32-34, 39-40; Romans 8:14-17; Matthew 28:16-20

An Unholy Distance

The heavenly honorific of today's feast puts me in mind of the teacher who told her six-year-olds to write to God and ask him a question. I'm sure he smiled at Jeannie's. She wrote, 'Dear God, in bible times did they really talk that fancy?'

Jesus never spoke 'fancy' about his Father. So, why should we? Two possibilities come to mind. First, we want to be reverential. The problem here, however, is that the language we use when 'reverential' can be all head and no heart. Consequently, we put God at a distance he neither wants nor observes. Love draws, it doesn't repel. So, if we call God a trinity, how can we love an abstraction?

Second, we don't have a clue who, or what, God is. This may be truer than we feel comfortable admitting. So we resort to abstraction. Now for some peculiar reason the more abstractly you present something the more profound some people think you are. I tend to think the opposite. It's only when you know something inside out that you can describe it simply. Profundity and simplicity go hand-in-hand, not profundity and abstraction – unless, of course, God can be reduced to a mathematical equation.

So how then to talk of God? Well, if the purpose is to reveal God in some way, talk is not the best way to go about it. Example is. Just as surely as talk of love can never replace the real thing, so 'trinity' can never replace the simplicity of Father, Son and the Love between them.

THE BODY AND BLOOD OF CHRIST

Readings: Exodus 24:3-8; Hebrews 9:11-15; Mark 14:12-16, 22:26

Not à la carte

Johnny got the message early in life. When asked by his religion teacher what he thought of God he replied with a gravity beyond his young years, 'I bet it's very hard for him to love all of everybody in the whole world. There are only four people in our family and I can never do it.' Out of the mouth of babes!

In today's first reading from the *Book of Exodus* the word 'all' is used repeatedly. In brief: all the people promise obedience to all the words of the Lord. There's no half measure, no *à la carte* approach to God's commands. There wasn't then, and there isn't now.

Today we celebrate the feast of The Body and Blood of Christ, or *Corpus Christi* as it's more popularly known. The Eucharist that Christ gave us is a meal open to all people who have committed themselves in faith to Jesus as Saviour.

The Eucharist, while it needs to be celebrated in a manner that expresses life, joy and community, is not an entertainment event. It's joyful yet serious, lively yet dignified, and in a sense 'ordinary' yet holy.

What we need to realise too, however, is that it also requires effort on our part to prepare for it and further effort to celebrate it well. That's where the 'all' comes in again. We can't prepare for the Eucharist with only part of our life. Following Jesus is a total life-long commitment. How could anyone celebrate Mass on a Sunday, having lived like a pagan on Saturday?

SECOND SUNDAY IN ORDINARY TIME

Readings: 1 Samuel 3:3-10, 19; 1 Corinthians 6:13-15, 17-20; John 1:35-42

Howls of Protest

This is something you may not want to hear. Even with faith in God it takes some getting used to. It's what Paul says in today's second reading: 'You are not your own.' You don't have the final say over what you can and can't do.

I can almost hear howls of protest from those who claim total ownership over themselves, from those who claim the 'right' to do whatever they wish provided it's not illegal, from those who claim the 'right' to end their life at a time and in a manner of their choosing – and generally from anybody who doesn't like being told what to do. And that covers a lot of people.

But isn't it basic to our faith that we belong to God, and are happy with that? Isn't that what baptism is about: acknowledging God's ownership of us? We didn't make ourselves, cause ourselves to be born, give ourselves life in any way whatsoever. So how can we possibly claim ownership over something we had no hand or act in making? We have been given as a gift unto ourselves – a gift for purpose not whimsy, for freedom not licence, forever not just for a day.

But suppose, for the sake of argument, that God's word in scripture were to tell us that God couldn't care less what we did here; that he couldn't be bothered whether we wiped ourselves off the face of the earth, for that matter, how would we feel?

I can almost hear howls of protest again.

THIRD SUNDAY IN ORDINARY TIME

Readings: Jonah 3:1-5, 10; 1 Corinthians 7:29-31; Mark 1:14-20

Revolutionary

Paul makes more strange statements this week. Take today's second reading, 'Let those who have wives be as though they had none, and those who mourn as though they were not mourning.' He's convinced that the age in which he lives is ending. He's right in one sense, and wrong in another.

He's wrong if he means the end of the world in terms of chronological time. He's right if he means the end of this world for the Christian in terms of its ways and values. That has a ring to it that needs to be heard every bit as urgently today as it did in Paul's time in Corinth.

In fact, in today's gospel reading we have Jesus preaching just that as his first public proclamation in Mark's gospel: 'The time is fulfilled, and the kingdom of God has come near; repent, and believe in the good news.'

Note the sequence here. Repent first; then believe. Clearly, acceptance of the news that Jesus brings as good is not possible without a change of heart and mind. And what is that news? Well, at this stage it's the fact that the kingdom of God is at hand. Later, in the light of Jesus' resurrection it becomes clear that entry into that kingdom brings resurrected life: new, full and everlasting.

When, like Paul, we believe that such a destiny can be ours then we'll look on this present world as passing, and act accordingly. Counter-cultural is what some people call it. Revolutionary is what I'd say it is!

FOURTH SUNDAY IN ORDINARY TIME

Readings: Deuteronomy 18:15-20; 1 Corinthians 7:32-35; Mark 1:21-28

Netting a Fisherman

Jesus' choice for 'pope' – like his teaching in today's gospel reading – is astounding: an unlettered fisherman. His followers were quick to change the gene pool. Had he made a mistake? Unlikely! Was Peter a failure? Hardly! So, why the shift? Who can say!

However, the 'why' of Jesus' choice is clear. No doubt there were intellectuals, academics and doctors of the Law around when Jesus lived. Yet these were not God's choice. God has the disconcerting habit of choosing unlikely people to do his work: Abraham and Sarah, Moses, David, the prophets, Job, Zachariah and Elizabeth, Mary and Joseph. The rationale being that it's God's power that must shine through what is being done, not the brilliance of the person doing it.

Jesus was a carpenter, not a scholar. None of his disciples was a scholar either. God's choice to get the ball rolling, if you'll pardon the expression, was unlettered people. I wonder how the church would have developed had we had tradesmen as popes instead of scholars. As the prospect of ever having such a pope again is remote – though knowing who's behind the scenes not impossible – harbouring such a thought seems ludicrous. Yet the question is valid.

How different would Christ's church be today had persons with trades under their belt instead of letters after their names been leading her? This speculation is interesting and useful for it brings to focus the biblical imperative that regardless of who leads, God is head. His power must shine through those who lead. Astounding, isn't it!

FIFTH SUNDAY IN ORDINARY TIME

Readings: Job 7:1-4, 6-7; 1 Corinthians 9:16-19, 22-23; Mark 1:29-39

Bad Will Hunting

The street-wise say that God created man in his own image and likeness, and then man returned the compliment. The incident in today's gospel reading, where Simon and his companions go out 'hunting' for Jesus, reminds me of that quip. The Greek verb used in verse 36 is *katadiókó*. A very strong word, it usually implies a hostile intent. So, 'hunting down' Jesus more accurately conveys what Simon was doing.

While people slept, Jesus made his way unhindered by the darkness to a deserted place to pray. People considered such places, devoid of human beings, as abodes of demons. Having just cast out many demons he now follows them to their dwelling. He has no fear. No evil can touch him. For Jesus, even an abode of evil is a place for prayer! That's a powerful and dramatic message: there are no God-free or prayer-free zones in life.

Back to the hunt again. Why would Simon want to hunt down Jesus? Well, he has just left everything to follow him, and now Jesus has disappeared. This doesn't fit the image of Jesus that Simon has. Finding him gone in the morning is a shock. This is the first time it has happened. What does it mean? Has Jesus run off? Is he a fraud, or a loony? Has Simon made one awful fool of himself in abandoning his livelihood for him? So, in doubt, frustration, and anger he sets out to find him. He's looking for Jesus, but on his own terms.

Does that ring a bell?

SIXTH SUNDAY IN ORDINARY TIME

Readings: Leviticus 13:1-2, 44-46; 1 Corinthians 10:31-11:1; Mark 1:40-45

Compassion through Anger

There are two possible images of Jesus in today's gospel reading. The obvious one is the compassionate Jesus who pities a leper and cures him. But then, why the 'stern warning'? It's not a warning to keep quiet, because that order comes after the stern warning. There's no information on what Jesus warns him about. Hence, the excuse to speculate.

The NRSV Catholic Edition has a footnote to v 41 stating that 'other ancient authorities read anger'. That's anger instead of pity. This makes more sense in terms of the 'stern warning'. The NRSV also notes that the terms leper and leprosy can refer to several diseases. Could the leper's disease be caused by a particular lifestyle? Jesus, recognising this, perhaps is angry with him. Yet, he cures him. Curing a leper who through no fault of his own contracts the disease warrants compassion. But Jesus' compassion could be even greater than that because he shows compassion to someone who possibly contracted a disease through his own fault. This is an even greater challenge for us today for it clearly shows that anger and compassion are not mutually exclusive. And that giving a stern warning about risky lifestyles is not out of order.

Could those who fashioned the final form of Mark's gospel have opted for the softer Jesus? If they did, what criteria did they use for their preference? And if they did were they correct? Could they have had difficulty with compassion flowing through anger?

It's an issue we too may have to face.

SEVENTH SUNDAY IN ORDINARY TIME

Readings: Isaiah 43:18-19,21-22, 24-25; 2 Corinthians 1:18-22; Mark 2:1-12

The Bits We Miss

Today's first reading makes me wonder if God still raises up prophets, or even needs to. Isn't our society literate, our church organised, our liturgies regular, the word of God on tap, so to speak? So, what do we need a prophet for? Could it be for bits we miss?

When we listen to God's word what do we hear? Words about love so general, saccharine and predictable that they pose no challenge to anybody? Or, words that compel us to put faces on those we must love and see among them those we hate? Perhaps a prophet could help us profile those ones. Words about God that place him way out there; remote, impersonal, and uncaring? Or, words that enable us to reach God way in here within our heart? If that's too close for comfort perhaps a prophet could tell us why. Words about having died with Christ in baptism, full of imagery but nothing else and soon forgotten? Or, words of power to radically change our way of life? Perhaps a prophet could supply that power. Words about a new heaven and new earth on their way, but with luck not today? Or, words that pump our hearts with hope and joy? Perhaps a prophet could provide the pump.

Yes, we do need prophets: those who have heard God's word and taken it to heart. Those who are comfortable with God up close and personal. Those who don't need to tell others what to do. Those who proclaim truth simply by the way they live.

EIGHTH SUNDAY IN ORDINARY TIME

Readings: Hosea 2:16-17, 21-22; 2 Corinthians 3:1-6; Mark 2:18-22

A Friendly Form of Virtual Reality

It's now a commodity. Friendship, that is. A company set up over a year ago to facilitate the renting of friends already has a data base of some 218,000 men and women ready for friendship at a moment's notice and an hourly rate. They accompany total strangers to restaurants, cinemas and art galleries, go shopping with them, and make small talk, utter soothing words, or give friendly advice – all for an agreed fee, of course. Already in cities in the US and Canada, the company has extended its services to the UK.

These neatly packaged, emotionally sanitised, no-strings-attached encounters are a far cry from that in today's first reading from Hosea. God has no interest in a rent-a-friend relationship. Our relationship with God must be free, personal, intimate and total. God doesn't deal in virtual reality.

The Lord's language here, 'I am going to lure her … and speak to her heart', as with that of the prophet Jeremiah, 'You have seduced me and I allowed myself to be seduced' (Jer 20:7) is boldly intimate. It's not the type of word we might expect to come from God even through the mouthpiece of a prophet. There's nothing indecisive, anaemic or platonic here. It's decidedly virile, robust and full-blooded. It's sincere; and the relationship it seeks is for keeps.

Not everybody wants, or can take, that type of relationship even with another human being – but even more so when it's with God. However, until, like Jeremiah, we allow ourselves to be seduced, God will be more virtual than real in our lives.

NINTH SUNDAY IN ORDINARY TIME

Readings: Deuteronomy 5:12-15; 2 Corinthians 4:6-11; Mark 2:23-3:6

Out of the Mouths of Babes

Babies are born hardwired for fair play. So a developmental psychologist at Yale University claims. Experiments with toddlers indicate this. For example, a group of one-year-olds watched three puppets at play. Let's call them A, B and C. A threw a yellow ball to B who caught it and playfully threw it back. C, however, grabbed the ball and ran off with it. Puppet B and C then appeared before the toddlers and a pile of sweets was put beside each puppet. The toddlers were told to take a sweet away from one puppet. Most took the sweet from C, the 'bold' puppet. A few even gave him a clip on the ear to boot. It seems they were just doing a-what-comes-naturally.

It's natural to rest when tired. But we don't always do so. Various factors can short-circuit our common sense: the pressure of a deadline, so many things to do yet so little time in which to do them. Even though common sense tells us that the time to relax is when we don't have time for it, we ignore that bit of hardwiring in our system.

Here, our faith helps. Today's first reading tells us to step back from life's hustle and bustle one day in seven. That day is set aside for two things: rest and God. In our highly secularised society that doesn't make sense. Developing an ulcer, or inviting a heart attack seems preferable.

If rest and prayer go out the door so too does freedom. If we don't play fair with God, we become a pressurised puppet on a string. Even a toddler can see that!

TENTH SUNDAY IN ORDINARY TIME

Readings: Genesis 3:9-15; 2 Corinthians 4:13-5:1; Mark 3:20-35

Passing the Buck

God blamed Adam. Adam blamed Eve. Eve blamed the serpent. The serpent didn't have a leg to stand on. In a quirky sort of a way that's part of what today's first reading from Genesis is telling us: we're great at passing the buck. And to save anyone the trauma of an apoplectic attack of moral outrage at the nerve of Adam and Eve to blame a third party for their transgression it's worthwhile bearing a few things in mind.

First, God declared his creation 'very good' only after he had created Adam and Eve. Second, he created them in his own image and likeness; therefore they were intrinsically good, even very good. Third, evil did not arise spontaneously from within human beings but originated from a source outside of them, symbolised by the serpent. Therefore, they were correct in blaming the serpent – at least in part.

So too with everyone who sins. Something external to them seduces them into acting in a manner below their nature. It would be rare for someone to choose evil for evil's sake. I'm not denying that someone could be sick enough, or eventually become evil enough, to do so. But reaching that stage of degeneracy takes time and commitment. Thank God, it's rare!

God doesn't fault Adam and Eve for passing the buck. But he does explain the facts of life to them. What they do has consequences. God is not to be trifled with. If prohibitions exist they exist for a reason. Part of growing up is learning and accepting the reasons for prohibitions.

We may be god-like in some ways, but we are not gods in any way.

ELEVENTH SUNDAY IN ORDINARY TIME

Readings: Ezekiel 17:22-24; 2 Corinthians 5:6-10; Mark 4:26-34

Mirror Image

Disney has finally done it. It has brought eternal youth to aging actors, even if only on screen. New computer technology it has developed can slough off the years from any antediluvian actor by capturing and mimicking their skin and muscle movement. It can process the imagery in such a way that they look as if they were just fresh from the mint and in their prime. Jeff Bridges is the first actor ever to play opposite a younger version of himself in the film *TRON: Legacy*.

But, apart from entertainment value, what use is that? We don't live on screen, or in virtual reality. I suppose for many the alternative to wrinkling naturally is selective slicing. The US alone saw 12.5 million cosmetic procedures performed in 2009 at a cost of $10 billion. It makes you wonder what has happened to the reality of aging gracefully. The aging can't be the problem because it's effortless. It must be the graceful part that's the problem.

Errant thoughts like these come to mind on hearing today's first reading from the prophet Ezekiel, especially the last lines saying that the Lord is he who stunts tall trees and makes low ones grow, who withers green trees and make withered ones green. A healthy relationship with God won't prevent wrinkles, but it will provide the grace.

Anyway, what's wrong with wrinkles? Don't they perform an important service in reminding us – especially those of us who fear, or are in denial of, our mortality – that the end is nigh, and unavoidable? Why wait until it's too late to find that out?

TWELFTH SUNDAY IN ORDINARY TIME

Readings: Job 3:1, 8-11; 2 Corinthians 5:14-17; Mark 4:35-41

A New Creation

Today's second reading states: 'If anyone is in Christ, there is a new creation: everything old has passed away; see everything has become new.' It reminds me of something St Augustine said about restless hearts. This verse seems to refer to a sudden transformation rather than a gradual evolution. God's Spirit operates to an urgency that nature doesn't. There's urgency as the Spirit hears nature's labour pains and our own inward groaning as we await adoption, the redemption of our bodies (Rom 8:23).

Do we feel that urgency ourselves? Well, that depends on how we look at things. Take, for example, the plans we make – whatever they may be. We're hoping for something better, be it home improvement, or job improvement, even self-improvement; or be it planning a holiday, buying a car, or something for the kids.

There's a constant 'wanting' in us for something new that we might blame consumerism for. Compulsive buying might be the outcome of the 'wanting', but at source the wanting is something deep and profound. It's nothing other than the yearning for the redemption of our bodies that Paul speaks of. It's our craving not just for better things, but more so for the best possible of all things: new creation, being transformed into the liberated children of God.

Back to St Augustine who put it so famously: 'You have made us for yourself, O Lord, and our hearts are restless until they rest in you.' Resting in God is not guaranteed to happen automatically. It's a journey we must make. And as we don't know how long we have to make the journey, every minute counts.

THIRTEENTH SUNDAY IN ORDINARY TIME

Readings: Wisdom 1:13-15, 2:23-24; 2 Corinthians 8:7, 9, 13-15; Mark 5:21-43

Made for Life

One venomous description of a gossip I came across recently was: someone who won't tell a lie if the truth can do more damage. Yet I suspect that today's first reading refers to that type of thing in some way when it tells us that God did not make death and does not delight in the death of the living. Our God is he who creates and loves life, who sends his son so that we may have life in its fullness (John 10:10). Realising that we are made in God's image, we too should not 'make death' nor delight in the death of anyone – not just in their physical death, but in anything that diminishes the quality of their life.

Every day we have life and death in our hands, in a manner of speaking. We can raise up, or bring down. We can praise, or criticise. We can work with, or plot against. We can bring joy, or instil fear. We can have people love us, or hate us. The choice is ours.

Temperament has a lot to do with this, but not everything. Much depends on our awareness and our generosity. Somebody once remarked that since we have to look someway it might as well be happy. So too, since we have to speak someway it might as well be positively.

There is so much gloom and doom around at times, you'd wonder if we really realise in whose image and likeness we're made: the God of life and creativity.

FOURTEENTH SUNDAY IN ORDINARY TIME

Readings: Ezekiel 2:2-5; 2 Corinthians 12:7-10; Mark 6:1-6

Beyond Reasonable Doubt

There's some strange stuff in today's gospel. Jesus, an unmarried 30-year-old, unlettered carpenter very forwardly starts to teach in his local synagogue. From his listeners' stunned reaction it must have been his first time to do so. You'd expect them to be indignant at his self-promoting posturing in the synagogue, as they'd see it, and to sneer at what he says. But no! They're impressed, amazed even, at his wisdom. In fact, so impressed are they that they just can't believe it. They can't get their head around the fact that someone like him – an ordinary Joe Soap of a carpenter – could have so much more than they have. Jealousy rears its ugly head, and instead of opening their minds to his wisdom they close their hearts to his person.

That's not all. He could do no deed of power there except to cure some people who were sick. They distanced themselves from him and would not allow him to work the miracle: personal transformation.

What this episode shows is that knowing about Jesus is not enough. We have to know him for the wonder to work. The miracle of transformation is a two-way thing: God and man at work together. We see Jesus in his humanity, but acknowledge him in his divinity too. As with those from his hometown, familiarity with the home-grown Jesus can breed contempt. We need to delve deeply, to go boldly where reason cannot take us.

Faith consists in believing when it is beyond the power of reason to discover.

FIFTEENTH SUNDAY IN ORDINARY TIME

Readings: Amos 7:12-15; Ephesians 1:3-14; Mark 6:7-13

Stretched out

Depending on your viewpoint it's refreshing, or alarming, how certain Paul can be in his statements on complex issues. Take today's second reading, for example. Here he just baldly states that God 'chose us in Christ before the foundation of the world to be blameless before him in love,' and that he 'made known the mystery of his will ... as a plan for the fullness of time'. Clearly, for him, God took great care with us humans, his creation.

Two things are striking here: his reference to God's pre-creation will and, for want of a better expression, his post-temporal one. Again, for Paul human beings are not an after-thought in the mind of God. No! Even before creation's foundation is set, way before any humans appear on the scene God already has a plan for them – and a great one at that! This seemingly quirky creation, queerer, and more chaotic than we can ever imagine, progresses according to a divine plan.

Here we feel the power of faith at work. For only faith can work at this level. Science has nothing to say about pre-foundational creation, about the awesome void of our pre-pyrotechnic cosmos, about the deafening silence of its final destination eerily dwarfing even the Big Bang's birth cry.

Yet here we have unscientific Paul opening our minds to realities that only faith can reveal, and stretching them to their limits, and then some. Are we ready for the strain of trying to comprehend God, small as a loving father yet enormous enough to encompass creation?

SIXTEENTH SUNDAY IN ORDINARY TIME

Readings: Jeremiah 23:1-6; Ephesians 2:13-18; Mark 6:30-34

Silence

In *The World of Silence,* Max Picard writes, 'And yet sometimes all the noise of the world today seems like the mere buzzing of insects on the broad back of silence.' There's something substantial about silence. Often people describe it as 'heavy'. Silence is formidable, even intimidating, if you're not friendly with it. But to be friendly with it, first you have to be friendly with you. One way of finding out if you are, is to go off to a lonely spot and see how long you can stay there before unease sets in.

How many people follow Jesus' advice to his disciples in today's gospel to go to a deserted place for peace and quiet? Are they not more inclined to go to a noisy holiday resort where's there's lots of action, lots of people, lots of things to do to fill the gap, lots of ways to forget oneself? Is there not something desperate about having to have a good time, and worse yet to feel obliged to say you had, even though you may not have had?

Getting used to silent, solitary periods to relax, to refresh our spirit, and take stock of our life is worthwhile. It helps us to think about important things that in the normal course of a day we rarely think of. Things like: life and its purpose, values we live by, people we hold precious, ambitions that drive us, the place we give to God in our life.

Silence is necessary not for finding answers but for finding questions.

SEVENTEENTH SUNDAY IN ORDINARY TIME

Readings: 2 Kings 4:42-44; Ephesians 4:1-6; John 6:1-15

In Need of Friends

Someone once pointed out that the best time to make friends is before you need them. Paul's passionate plea for unity in today's second reading is a reminder of that fact. Paul, of course, doesn't package his plea in such self-serving terms. However, in its own street-wise fashion the remark is true. Unity is good, disunity is not. It's as simple as that.

Paul uses language here that many people, particularly men perhaps, may find difficult to identify with in terms of relating to others. He pleads for 'humility', 'gentleness', 'patience' and that awful thing called 'love'. In an age when, in the name of so-called entertainment, we are bombarded with images of just the opposite of these – anger, hate, violence, and abuse – we might be pardoned for wondering which is the norm in life: humility or arrogance, gentleness or aggression, patience or frenzy, love or hate. A constant diet of grim actors on TV, and on the screen, aping antisocial antics as if life consisted of never-ending rows fuelled by mindless jealousy can result in a build up of bile.

So, whether we suffer from indigestion or not is up to us. Which do we want: to be hurtful or helpful, coarse or courteous, aggressive or friendly? Those who feed on anger, hate and violence are no strangers to fear. These take more out of us than they give. It's the caring, the friendship and the love that makes life pleasant and fulfilling.

Ask any angry, jealous and friendless role model you can find.

EIGHTEENTH SUNDAY IN ORDINARY TIME

Readings: Exodus 16:2-4, 12-15; Ephesians 4:17, 20-24; John 6:24-35

The New Self

Thomas Merton wrote in *Contemplation in a World of Action*: 'The new man is not just the old man in possession of a legal certificate entitling him to a reward.' That's not the 'new self' Paul refers to in today's second reading. So, what is it?

First, what it isn't. It isn't living as the Gentiles live 'in the futility of their minds'. In other words, it's not living as if you only had your own mind to depend on. Using only that to comprehend life is futile. It's a dead end trip. Removed from the light of God's word the human mind becomes dark, the human heart becomes hard, and human behaviour degenerates into debauchery. Paul wasn't warning about what might happen, he was describing what already had happened.

Were we to think that reason reigns supreme – pristine and pure – and confine ourselves to its limits deprived of the light of God's word, and the power of his Spirit would our understanding and behaviour not deteriorate too? Could we even speak of deterioration of behaviour at all? For if nothing greater than a mind exists, who's to say that yours is any better than mine? My mind, not yours, sets my standards. As Hamlet says, 'There is nothing either good or bad but thinking makes it so' – my thinking, that is.

The new self, however, recognises that God sets the standards and it lives by them 'in true righteousness and holiness'. The new man, the new self, is the one who is righteous and holy before God.

NINETEENTH SUNDAY IN ORDINARY TIME

Readings: 1 Kings 19:4-8; Ephesians 4:30-5:2; John 6:41-51

Difficult Word

Today we have another strange reading from Paul. He warns the Ephesians not 'to grieve the Holy Spirit of God' by bitterness, wrath, anger, wrangling, slander and malice. Instead they should be kind, tenderhearted, and forgiving. That's fine.

But then he describes Christ's giving himself up for us, i.e. surrendering to death, as a 'fragrant offering and sacrifice to God'. I find it difficult to grasp that Paul should consider the Spirit upset by human malice, yet the Father pleased by his Son's death in facing up to that malice. Why does malice aggrieve the Holy Spirit if not because of the damage it does to both victim and perpetrator? Why then does the suffering it inflicts on God's Son not aggrieve that Spirit too? At least, if it does Paul doesn't say so.

Reading Paul one way gives the impression that the Father was pleased with both the suffering and the love that enabled Jesus to face his suffering and death. Reading him another way gives the impression, intended or not, that the Father wanted his Son to suffer on our behalf – hence the fragrance of the sacrifice. However, this seriously compromises God's compassionate nature as revealed in the parable of the prodigal son. Then reading Paul a third way gives the impression that the fragrance is in Paul's nostrils, not the Father's. If true, this simplifies matters. It's Paul's view of Jesus' suffering and death, not God's.

Scripture at times can be really difficult to understand, and the word of God it contains difficult to hear.

TWENTIETH SUNDAY IN ORDINARY TIME

Readings: Proverbs 9:1-6; Ephesians 5:15-20; John 6:51-58

Cop on or Cop out

The message on the church bulletin board reads: 'Those who stand for nothing fall for everything.' Wisdom is knowing what to stand for – and standing up for it. Wisdom is putting knowledge to good use. Today's first reading urges us to 'lay aside immaturity, and live and walk in the way of insight'. Easier said than done.

Someone who is immature is not ripe. Growth in one or more areas of their life slowed down or stopped completely at some stage. It's scary enough that such a thing can happen, but to make matters worse it can happen without our realising it until it's late in the day.

Today's reading also tells us to walk in the way of insight. Fine! But how do you do that? You can't just decide to have an insight as you'd have a cup of tea. You can't conjure one up, order one over the Internet, or go to a shop and buy one. No! They either come to you or they don't. However, maybe it's just one basic insight that the reading refers to. Once you've had that one, others follow of their own accord as life presents them. But without the basic one you miss the others. And what more basic to realise than that life has purpose, and consequences that extend beyond death. Once that sinks in we begin to see things differently.

Wisdom has built her house, set her pillars, and prepared a meal for those who enter. So let's put immaturity aside and live. Let's cop on not cop out.

TWENTY-FIRST SUNDAY IN ORDINARY TIME

Readings: Joshua 24:1-2, 15-18; Ephesians 5:21-32; John 6:60-69

Take it or Leave it

There's very much a take-it-or-leave-it approach evident in today's gospel reading. There's no attempt at gentle persuasion. Jesus has just told the Jews that he is the living bread from heaven and that anyone who eats it will live forever. Does he think that the Jews will jump for joy at hearing this? Strangely, instead of laughing him to scorn, or just turning their back on him as a crackpot, as you might expect, they dispute among themselves about what he means. Now why would they do that? Why would they take seriously someone who makes so outlandish a claim?

Two reasons perhaps. First, there's something about Jesus that demands he be taken seriously, no matter what. There's an intensity of presence, charisma, and power in him that tells you he's not the type to make nonsensical statements. Whatever about his statements being enigmatic, you know they can never be idiotic. Therefore, the Jews take him seriously and try to understand him.

Second reason: his works. Jesus has publicly performed works of extraordinary power. Miracles we call them. Because we've not experienced directly such works ourselves we cannot fully appreciate their effect. Just imagine if you witnessed someone performing even one of the healings attributed to Jesus would you not be totally gobsmacked? Would you not take seriously every utterance of such a person?

Jesus presents his followers with a take-it-or-leave-it claim. Why? Because if what he has done does not convince, then words won't either. As St Francis noted, we should preach the gospel at all times, using words when necessary.

TWENTY-SECOND SUNDAY IN ORDINARY TIME

Readings: Deuteronomy 4:1-2, 6-8; James 1:17-18, 21-22, 27; Mark 7:1-8, 14-15, 21-23

Give-and-take

To paraphrase Benjamin Disraeli: There are rules, damned rules and commandments. Whatever about the rules, damned or otherwise, the commandments must be observed diligently according to today's first reading. Doing so shows wisdom and discernment. What a pleasant and peaceful way of looking at someone else's orders to you! Not characteristic of today's ethos. I wonder what goes wrong to give the impression that God's commandments are burdens to be borne, better yet ignored, rather than gifts to be cherished.

Why do some people worship money, power and sex instead of the one true God? Why can't they see the tyranny that servitude to these produces? Why can't they see the freedom that having only the one true God in one's life endows? And why can't they see God's commandments as guiding lights to help them travel life's convoluted course in safety? There are so many 'whys.'

God created us to live in community. At family level community living calls for give-and-take. If members make demands regardless of how it affects others, then the quality of life degrades. If all are equally demanding, then you have a dysfunctional family.

At world level, community living also calls for give-and-take: individually, collectively, and nationally. God's commandments wise us up to the need for justice, generosity, and respect for all people. They help us to adapt to life out there in the real world. They prevent us from expecting that life to adapt to us. That's why many don't like them. But, if we didn't have them, would we not have to invent them?

TWENTY-THIRD SUNDAY IN ORDINARY TIME

Readings: Isaiah 35:4-7; James 2:1-5; Mark 7:31-37

One for all

Today's gospel reading contains a string of strange things. For starters, how could someone deaf from birth, presumably, be able to speak at all, even with an impediment? There were no books then, no special-needs teaching. Nothing. So how did he pick up a language? No answer is given. Not one for theatricals, Jesus nevertheless uses gestures common at the time to Greek and Jewish healers. Why? No reason is given. Equally strange, he imposes silence on the crowd after the healing. Could he really expect them to keep quiet about such an extraordinary thing? No explanation is given.

There are no answers to these questions. Yet, asking them helps us focus on the text to grasp its style and purpose. It's penned not as a report for a newspaper, but for the purpose of teaching. It tells us that lots of good things happen when we're close to Jesus. We become whole and free in a way we've never been before. Our damaged humanity is healed.

It also tells us important things about Jesus in an indirect way. The crowds proclaim that he has 'done everything well'. This is reminiscent of Gen 1:31: 'God saw everything that he had made and indeed it was very good.' There's at least a linkage with God's divine action here. And because the healing occurs in the Gentile region, east of Jordan, it tells us that the Gentiles, previously deaf and dumb to God, can now hear and respond to him.

Jesus is for all, not just the chosen few.

TWENTY-FOURTH SUNDAY IN ORDINARY TIME

Readings: Isaiah 50:5-9; James 2:14-18; Mark 8:27-35

The Cross Section

We face the cross again in today's gospel. 'If any want to become my followers, let them deny themselves and take up their cross and follow me.' We're not allowed to forget the cross for long, are we? I wonder, though, did Jesus actually use the expression 'take up their cross'. If, as presented, he were talking directly to the crowd would he not have said 'you' instead of 'any', and 'yourselves' instead of 'themselves'? But maybe that's a translation issue. Maybe. Was the expression 'take up your cross' common coinage then? Is it not more likely to have been a later Christian expression in the light of Jesus' death and resurrection?

However, what is important is that Jesus – and consequently us his followers – was not a pain seeker. Suffering for suffering's sake is sick. Suffering for a purpose is not. Jesus' death on the cross is not a justification for us to seek pain. We're not masochists. But neither do we avoid the cross when it blocks the path to follow Jesus.

Jesus links crosses with following him. To follow him is the reason for carrying them. But not just carrying them; using them, in fact, to serve his mission of bringing his good news to those who need to hear it. Part of that good news is that love is greater than fear, that the spirit to serve God's kingdom is stronger than the urge to preserve vested interests.

We never have to go dial a cross. The true one is always with us.

TWENTY-FIFTH SUNDAY IN ORDINARY TIME

Readings: Wisdom 2:12, 17-20; James 3:16-4:3; Mark 9:30-37

Hobson's Choice?

Today's gospel reading makes you wonder what on earth possessed Jesus to choose the ones he did to become his disciples. He's teaching them vitally important matters but not only do they not understand what he's saying, they're afraid even to ask him what he means. Why? Could they fear that he may tire of them and look for others more intelligent to replace them as his disciples?

Though slow on the uptake, they're quick on the draw. Self-seeking calculation has them bickering about which of them is top dog. Not only are they a bit dense, they're also small-time glory seekers. Could any group of people be less likely candidates to become Jesus' disciples?

Yet, he chose them knowing their calibre and knowing what he was doing. Amazing! Even more amazing is the change in them after Jesus' death and resurrection, a change that sees them proclaiming a most profound message and establishing a faith-community that has spread throughout the world down to this present day. It was also a change that produced in them total commitment to God, even to the point of death.

Bringing it closer to home, is it not equally amazing the type of people God still calls today to do his work? I don't mean priests and religious primarily but parents. What more precious task could be entrusted to a human being than to bring another into this world and introduce them to God?

We too can be dense and self-seeking, yet God has chosen us. How has the gift of life changed us?

TWENTY-SIXTH SUNDAY IN ORDINARY TIME

Readings: Numbers 11:25-29; James 5:1-6; Mark 9:38-43, 45, 47-48

PS: I thank you!

I came across a prayer some time ago that caught my attention. Can't remember where, but here's the prayer: 'Dear God, we rejoice and give thanks for earthworms, bees, ladybirds and broody hens; for humans tending their gardens, talking to animals, cleaning their homes and singing to themselves; for the rising of the sap, the fragrance of growth, the invention of the wheelbarrow and the existence of the teapot, we give thanks. We celebrate and give thanks. Amen.'

In light of today's readings that prayer makes me ask how often I give thanks to God for the fine things that others do – especially if they seem to be muscling in on my turf. Jealousy is often quicker off the mark than generosity. But not always.

In today's readings Moses and Jesus wish that everyone be filled with God's Spirit. The more that Spirit is active in our world the better. It doesn't matter through whom the Spirit works. Criticising someone for doing good is like telling the Holy Spirit whom he may work with. Now that would be arrogant.

In 1 Cor 13:4 Paul writes: '... love is not envious or boastful or arrogant or rude'. If we love it will not be as an afterthought, as a *PS: I love you*. If we are happy to acknowledge God's freedom to do as he wishes and choose whom he will for his purpose, then neither will our thanks be a mere afterthought, a *PS: I thank you!*

TWENTY-SEVENTH SUNDAY IN ORDINARY TIME

Readings: Genesis 2:18-24; Hebrews 2:9-11; Mark 10:2-16

Made in Heaven?

Here's a piece of worldly wisdom: A man is incomplete until he's married; then when he is, he's finished! In other words: marriage makes or breaks. The Pharisees in today's gospel reading are aware of this too when they ask Jesus if it's lawful for a man to divorce his wife. Note that it's the legal aspect of marriage they focus on to test him – not a respectful attitude to Jesus or the Law. Law's purpose is to guide, not to entrap. So, too, with God's word.

Today it guides us to an understanding of marriage between a man and a woman as a relationship that lasts. This may be hard to take. So a few questions: if divorce is good for society then should it not be on call? Why limit it to just once or twice? If people who marry want the divorce option down the line should this not be expressed in the marriage ceremony? How could someone marrying, who wants divorce as an option, promise 'to have and to hold for better or for worse until death us do part'? To be honest would they not have to declare: 'to have and to hold for better but not for worse and until one of us decides to divorce'? But who would want to begin their life together saying that in public? Could love be so calculating?

If it could, then perhaps a comment on marriage that the *Readers Digest* carried many years ago might still be true: marriage is an illusion and a snore!

TWENTY-EIGHTH SUNDAY IN ORDINARY TIME

Readings: Wisdom 7:7-11; Hebrews 4:12-13; Mark 10:17-30

Bargain Basement Wisdom

A wise man once wrote for his gravestone: 'As I am now, you soon shall be, so be content to follow me.' When he died, a wiser one taped a note to it that read: 'To follow you I'm not content, until I know which way you went!' Ah! That's wisdom.

Wisdom is applying truth to the art of living. The truth comes free in the word of God but applying it comes at a price. Today's second reading marks the price: having our soul and spirit, our joints and marrow separated by something sharper than any two-edged sword. Not everyone wants to endure that. The rich man in today's gospel reading doesn't want to, and he loses out. He abandons Jesus and departs poorer than when he came even though his wealth remains intact. Not only does he leave the poorer, he leaves grieving.

Instinctively he knows that there's more to his life than wealth. Jesus' word pierces him like a two-edged sword, but he's unwilling to allow it to separate him from his wealth. He loses out. He knows it, yet still won't change. He wants wisdom; is offered it, but thinks the price is too high. He wants a bargain-basement type that just doesn't exist.

Change wealth to anything else we long for in the secret of our heart – anything that blocks our way to God. That's the spot God's word needs to hit, to separate us from it so that we come to possess wisdom because we've allowed God to possess us.

TWENTY-NINTH SUNDAY IN ORDINARY TIME
MISSION SUNDAY

Readings: Isaiah 53:10-11; Acts 13:14-49; Mark 10:42-45

Out of Reach

Three priests sat discussing the best positions for prayer while a telephone repairman worked nearby. 'Kneeling is definitely best,' claimed one. 'No,' said another. 'I get the best results standing with my hands outstretched to heaven.' 'You're both wrong,' the third insisted. 'The most effective prayer position is lying prostrate, face down on the floor.' The repairman could contain himself no longer. 'Hey, fellas,' he shouted, 'the best prayin' I ever did was hangin' upside down from a telephone pole.'

Not the first position you'd think of for prayer, but definitely one that works. Today's gospel reading describes another that works: that of servant. Not for prayer this time, but for mission. It makes the startling claim that the more we serve – even to becoming a slave of all – the more we advance as followers of Jesus, the closer we get to him in other words.

We don't follow him just for our own sakes. Being with him means taking on his mission: bringing people back to God. Jesus did this by his witness and proclamation, by what he did and said. So, too, must we because baptism makes us missionaries, confirmation primes us to begin, God's word fires us to set out and reach out to others.

Today we celebrate Mission Sunday, whose theme this year is *Reach Out*. So let's do just that. We can reach out wherever we are to whomever we wish. And the wonder is that by reaching out we come to see that no one is out of reach.

THIRTIETH SUNDAY IN ORDINARY TIME

Readings: Jeremiah 31:7-9; Hebrews 5:1-6; Mark 10:46-52

A Stupid Question?

Jesus doesn't ask stupid questions. So, why does he ask Bartimeus what seems at best a question with an obvious answer in today's gospel reading? Bartimeus is blind, and a beggar. He calls Jesus 'Son of David.' So the odds are in favour of him wanting more than money. He wants his sight. Yet, Jesus doesn't assume that. Why?

Perhaps he wants to show respect towards Bartimeus, unlike the crowd who tell him to shut up. Jesus invites him to speak for himself. Can we say we always do that with those we consider unimportant to us? Those whose sentences we finish for them? Those whose conversation we cut across when in company? Those whom we think aren't worth listening to?

Or perhaps Jesus wants to test the quality of Bartimeus's faith. 'Son of David' he calls Jesus. Will he now undo the impression he makes by asking Jesus for a few coins? Respecting Bartimeus's freedom, Jesus let's his faith unfold. And what a faith it is! He asks for nothing short of a miracle. Even though he's blind he can 'see' that Jesus is more than ordinary. Faith brings vision of a kind that healthy eyes may fail to. Do we see in Jesus more than the human eye can catch? Is our faith great enough to expect a personal transformation little short of the miraculous by sincerely asking for it? Jesus doesn't force us to ask for the impossible. But he does invite us to.

What a shame should we refuse because it might sound stupid!

THIRTY-FIRST SUNDAY IN ORDINARY TIME

Readings: Deuteronomy 6:2-6; Hebrews 7:23-28; Mark 12:28-34

A Kind of Love

There was no half-measures as far as a 49-year-old Belgian runner was concerned. Crossing seven countries, he ran 365 marathons in one year. That's 42.195km a day, every day, for 365 days. Doing so earned him a slot in the *Guinness Book of Records*. His success, he said, depended on taking things easy. His measured pace and four-hour average for each marathon enabled him to maintain a slow heartbeat.

Why did he do it? He didn't say. But he did admit that once, in Mexico, when the going was particularly tough he asked himself what on earth he was doing there. As a youngster he was asthmatic. Doctors told him to avoid sports. One wonders could this have had anything to do with it. Telling someone not to do something can be the best way of ensuring that they do it.

I wonder if such reverse logic works with loving God. Today's first reading and gospel tells us to love the Lord our God with all our heart, with all our soul and with all our strength. And for good measure the gospel extends such whole-hearted love to cover our neighbour.

Maybe it's the word 'love' that causes problems for most of us. Love implies feeling. Benign feeling, that is. We don't always have such feeling for our neighbour and can't summon it at will. So, to love whole-heartedly perhaps two options should be considered: forbid such love and see what happens, or think 'kindness instead of 'love'.

We might run from love, but not from kindness. And it keeps the heartbeat steady.

THIRTY-SECOND SUNDAY IN ORDINARY TIME

Readings: 1 Kings 17:10-16; Hebrews 9:24-28; Mark 12:38-44

The Widow's Mite

The widow's mite symbolises generosity. A small gesture bursting with meaning grabs the imagination and immortalises itself. Today's gospel reading notes that the widow has two coins. She could give one, keep the other, and still be considered generous. But no! Her generosity is not half measure. Her reverence for God and her respect for the Law and its requirements are total.

The spotlight is on the quality of her giving. We don't know what happens to her afterwards. But somehow we just know she's not going to die of starvation. We can't prove it, of course. But God doesn't respond to generosity with punishment. What kind of a god would that be!

It's the same for us. When we respond generously to life's demands we're not punished for doing so. Here are some more things we can't prove, but which are true nonetheless: the more we give the more we discover we have to give; and, not only are those who receive enriched, so too are those who give.

When I worked in Indonesia as a missionary occasionally I gave money to people in need, or spent it for medical treatment on their behalf. To my surprise, on several occasions I received money out of the blue from home in the form of Mass offerings within weeks of having given help to others. Like the jar of meal and the jug of oil in today's first reading my small jar was never empty either.

It really does work that way. Try it and see.

THIRTY-THIRD SUNDAY IN ORDINARY TIME

Readings: Daniel 12:1-13; Hebrews 10:11-14, 18; Mark 13:24-32

Beyond the Senses

There are only two possibilities: human life has meaning or it hasn't. It has direction powered by purpose, or else it's like a fungus, free-floating on a speck of cosmic dust going nowhere fast. But if there is nothing beyond what we see, touch, taste, hear and smell, from where comes the heart's deep yearning for things beyond the senses? Francis Thompson expresses that yearning in his poem, *In No Strange Land*:

O world invisible, we view thee
O world intangible, we touch thee
O world unknowable, we know thee
Inapprehensible, we clutch thee!

That clutching is for that which gives life its mystery, for that which shatters the daily deceit of seemingly ordinary things to grace us with a glimpse of their grandeur. It's palpable in music that captives the soul, in poetry that punctuates the mundane with rhythm from another zone. It's in art that sates the eye with beauty transcending time. It's in people when they love, and even when they don't.

When we're in touch with mystery today's first reading will not seem as bizarre as it might otherwise appear. Its style won't take from its substance. Resurrection of the dead is clearly central to God's plan for his creation.

We need to focus on resurrection else death will have the final say. And the spot for that focus is life's ordinary things. Again Francis Thompson:

Not where the wheeling systems darken
And our benumbed conceiving soars!
The drift of pinions, would we hearken
Beats at our own clay-shuttered doors.

OUR LORD JESUS CHRIST UNIVERSAL KING

Readings: Daniel 7:13-14; Apocalypse 1:5-8; John 18:33-37

Truth Reigns

Someone remarked that there are three sides to every story: your side, my side and the truth. In today's gospel reading Jesus links the reign of his kingdom very closely with testifying to truth. Celebrating Jesus as universal king, means celebrating truth's triumph over falsehood, the victory of good over evil.

However, lest triumphalism makes us cocky, we need to remember the cost of this triumph – nothing less than the torture and murder of God's Son on earth. Sounds a bit strange put that way, doesn't it? We're more used to hearing about the passion and death of Jesus. Passion has become a sanitised word, sounding less harsh than torture, even though the pain of it isn't. Crucifixion, while a terrible word and an even more terrible reality, still sounds that bit more distant than murder does.

Jesus was murdered because he spoke the truth. Anyone who speaks as Jesus did risks the same fate ultimately. Yet, in spite of threats from those with vested interests who don't want the truth to be told, truth will out and does prevail. That's what we celebrate this day. But, not only do we celebrate the victory of truth, we also celebrate the fact that people are prepared to die for it. We have examples of that throughout history. We have martyrs for truth among us today. We will have them into the future too.

Today we celebrate the three sides to this story: I testify to truth, you testify to truth and truth triumphs, for all three become one.

FIRST SUNDAY OF ADVENT

Readings: Jeremiah 33:14-16; 1 Thessalonians 3:12-4:2; Luke 21:25-28, 34-36

Caterpillars Beware!

What a way to enter with a bang! Enter a new liturgical year, that is. Just look at our second reading today: 'May the Lord make you increase and abound in love for one another and for all.' What a way to start the year if love means, as it must, seeing butterflies in caterpillars! Not even Specsavers could do that for you.

Advent is a time for staring: at the Creator coddled in a cot, at heaven harboured in a home, at power naked in swaddling clothes, at divinity bubbling through a baby, at the darkness of a silent night illumined by a cosmic chorus of heavenly hosannas. Indeed it is; but don't forget the caterpillar.

Why should we be stumped by a muddled Marian message ringed in a tree? Why have apparitions in strange places? Don't we have divinity at our fingertips each day? We need but reach out in friendship to another human being to touch the face of God. For if not there, where else?

Advent is a time for daring: to find the intimately elusive God nestling in our hearts, to find his sacred face imaged on the heart of those we love and, dare we admit it, those we don't; to trust our instincts for the promised paradise to come. Indeed it is, but don't forget the caterpillar.

Next time you meet one, stare and dare. Stare until its lowly form morphs before your eyes. Then dare to believe what your eyes tell you. Advent has arrived; can birth be far behind?

SECOND SUNDAY OF ADVENT

Readings: Baruch 5:1-9; Philippians 3:1-6, 8-11; Luke 3:1-6

On the Margins

Drunk and wobbling, he stood in the middle of O'Connell Street, Dublin. Ignoring the rictus of the floosie in the jacuzzi statue behind him, he berated passers-by for walking around in a dream and not knowing it. He had a point. But no impact. 'Ye'r all livin' in a dream!' was his shouted message. But for his spectral hearers the medium was the message: a noonday drunk couldn't have anything worthwhile to say.

Yet what about another down-and-out: the poet Francis Thompson. He had much to say, and all of it worthwhile. As God's word came to John the Baptist in the wilderness of sand (today's gospel) so too it came to an opium addict in his wilderness of streets. When it came his eyes opened and he penned these luminous lines:

The angels keep their ancient places
Turn but a stone and start a wing!
'Tis ye, 'tis your estrangèd faces,
That miss the many-splendoured thing.

John the Baptist couldn't have put it better! Truly what Advent announces is a 'many-splendoured thing': God's splendour shining through simplicity, God's power bursting through weakness. Conceived out of wedlock, born out of home, rejected by society, killed by the 'law', Jesus became a man on the margins.

Do we want to cheer at the birth of a marginalised man? Do we want to listen to what he says? Do we not prefer the hollow chant of 'Ho! Ho! Ho!' and the glint of tacky tinsel? Could that be why we've handed Christmas over to kids?

THIRD SUNDAY OF ADVENT

Readings: Zephaniah 3:14-18; Philippians 4:4-7; Luke 3:10-18

Pitch Battles

Had there been footballers in the days of John the Baptist what would he say to them if they came to him for advice, as those in today's gospel do? 'Play the man and keep your courage high'? (Joshua 1:18, depending on translation) Or, 'Leave your knives at home'? Maybe not then, but today he might have to if a recent newspaper report is true.

Footballers in France's amateur leagues are being encouraged to leave their knives, scissors and even pistols at home because of a riot of on-pitch violence. Of the 700,000 matches played in the 2007-08 season 12,000 had serious incidents of physical or verbal abuse. Hot-headed players, aka warm-hearted sportsmen, were responsible for 90 per cent of the violence, involving kicking (not the ball) punching and brawling.

Being a sportsman isn't easy, it seems. Being a thug comes easier. Doing what a Christian does isn't easy either: sharing food with those who have none, acting honestly in dealing with others, respecting them, and never bullying or being greedy. John the Baptist makes no extraordinary demands. Unburdened by degrees in theology, philosophy or psychology, or by diplomas from courses in spirituality, dream analysis or tree hugging, he knows instinctively – as most of us do – what's needed: generosity, honesty, and gentleness. These bring peace.

Christmas may ooze platitudinous peace. The real thing does not come cheap. Tinsel and mistletoe can never replace the word of God. That word brought Jesus to his death and resurrection. As we celebrate Advent let's ask: Where is it bringing me?

FOURTH SUNDAY OF ADVENT

Readings: Micah 5:1-4: Hebrews 10:5-10; Luke 1:39-44

Importance of Being Little

Size matters, even when it's small. Take, for example, the Galápagos islands. They're not small nor a problem but the mosquitoes brought there by chartered flights and tourist boats are. Getting its name from the Spanish for 'small fly', the 'mosquito is a real and present danger to the islands' unique species. Many mosquitoes carry deadly diseases such as avian malaria or West Nile fever. They could endanger even the Galápagos tortoises, marine iguanas, sea lions and Darwin's famous finches.

But small things can do much good too. Take, for example, bacteria. A controversial scientist trying to sequence the human genome (containing 3 billion DNA base pairs) claimed in August 2008 that by the end of 2009 artificial life would be produced in the lab. For some time now he has been trying to produce bacteria that would change coal into natural gas, and algae that would absorb carbon dioxide and turn it into hydrocarbon fuels. Small things can indeed have an enormous impact.

Today's first reading knows the value of small things too, for it foretells the impact that the emergence of a ruler of Israel from one of Judah's little clans will have. Repeatedly God chooses the small and insignificant in the world's eyes for very important missions.

Advent is a reminder that we, who for the most part are small and insignificant in the world's eyes, have been chosen for mission too. When at Christmas we celebrate that 'ruler's' birth let us be aware that in a very real sense we celebrate our own – our birth into greatness.

THE IMMACULATE CONCEPTION

Readings: Genesis 3:9-15, 20; Ephesians 1:3-6, 11-12; Luke 1:26-38

The Faith Move

Being all wired up may soon be a thing of the past. Thanks to a breakthrough in physics, inventors claim to have sent electricity wirelessly through the air. They hope to be able to charge laptops, mobile phones and television sets at home without having to plug them in to a socket. It may sound like starry-eyed Star Trek scenario but today's science fiction may be tomorrow's science fact.

Science's progress is so impressive that some people put their faith in science more easily than in religion. Ironically, one so aggressively atheistic as Richard Dawkins sees no nonsense in believing that there are 'very probably alien civilisations that are superhuman' (*The God Delusion,* p 98) without a shred of evidence to support it – while rubbishing belief in the existence of God. Faith in extra-terrestrials is fine. Faith in God is foolish.

But once you make the fundamental move to faith, things that otherwise might seem nonsensical fall into place. Today's feast is one of them. Mary, she who would be the mother of God's son, was uniquely united with God from the first instant of her existence: her conception. Nothing less would be appropriate. God smiled on her in a special way. She was born into his favour in a manner no other human had ever been. Any degree of alienation from God in the bearer of God is unthinkable. So too any form of bodily decay in the body that bore that life is equally unthinkable. The Immaculate Conception and the Assumption complement each other as logical extensions within a framework of faith.

CHRISTMAS DAY

Readings: Isaiah 52:7-10: Hebrews 1:1-6; John 1:1-18

The Intangibles

Apollo 8, launched on December 21, 1968, to orbit the Moon paved the way for the first human to set foot on its surface before the end of that decade. It made ten lunar orbits in 20 hours. However, it wasn't the Moon that captivated the crew but Mother Earth. From their seats in the gods, their eyes riveted on her spellbinding beauty, they made a Christmas Eve television broadcast. Timing it to coincide with a full view of the planet suspended in the empty blackness of infinite space, the crew read the first ten verses from the *Book of Genesis*. Up to then it was the most watched TV programme ever.

We're familiar now with the image of that big, beautiful orb wrapped in its gossamer covering of life-giving gases. This protective layer above all else stuns us into realizing how much life on earth with all its beauty, diversity and richness depends on something so ethereal as air. Our delicate, intangible atmosphere is vital for our physical survival.

So too are intangible things vital for our communal survival. Things like respect shown through courtesy to one another, and kindness shown in caring for each other. Things like thinking well of others so that we speak well of them and act decently towards them. Things like awareness of their and our relationship to God. Things like faith in that God and hope in his promise of a glorious destiny for humankind.

And, of course, Christmas Day to remind us of Jesus' birth and why, like the Magi, we fall down in adoration before him.

THE FEAST OF THE HOLY FAMILY

Readings: 1 Samuel 1:20-22, 24-28; 1 John 3:1-2, 21-24; Luke 2:41-52

Gift-wrapped from God

A news item in *The Irish Times* of 9 September 2009 caught my eye. It was headed, 'Couple marry at son's funeral.' It told of a couple from New York State who got married at their son's funeral. His name was Asa and he was only seven when killed. He was travelling as a passenger in his grandfather's car when it crashed in a multiple car pile up. His one wish in life was that his parents should marry. He had frequently asked them why they weren't. Strange that one so young could feel what was most appropriate while the adults concerned couldn't. Out of the mouth of babes ... (Ps 8:3).

In today's gospel reading another child also asks his parents a question. It too reveals what he finds most appropriate: that he be in his Father's house. Telling his parents that his place is in his Father's house confuses them. Even his mother, who presumably knows full well his extraordinary origins, doesn't grasp what he's implying or revealing about himself. This makes one wonder what the Annunciation actually was and what it conveyed to Mary.

Mary and Joseph had with them the One whom no human mind can fathom. So, if even they who are closest to him don't recognise who he is – and indeed how can they? – then we shouldn't be too disappointed at our inability to recognise him at times either.

This holds even for members of our own families. We may think we know them, but deep down they're a mystery gift-wrapped from God.

SECOND SUNDAY AFTER CHRISTMAS

Readings: Sirach 24:1-2, 8-12; Ephesians 1:3-6, 15-18; John 1:1-18

Born of God

The United States eased restrictions on sex selection of embryos in 2001. Since then 'medical tourism' for 'family balancing' has increased. The total cost of procedures, travel and accommodation to ensure the birth of a baby of the desired sex can reach €23,000. I wonder how much time, effort and money the parents subsequently spend on rearing the child to be 'holy and blameless before God in love'. Today's second reading tells us that God chose us – even before the foundation of the world – to be holy and blameless before him. That's God's choice and our calling, regardless of our sex. When being male or female becomes more important than being a person, then we've lost the run of ourselves.

As we evolve, and hopefully mature, on this planet and learn to control nature more and more, the challenge is to allow God to be God in our lives, i.e. to leave things in God's hands, to use an old-fashioned expression. Maybe even to leave anything in his hands. Why should we, when ours can do what we want them to do?

Apart from the moral issues involved in so much invasive procedure and its consequences where fertility and birth are concerned, such as the fate of embryos who don't pass muster to see the light of day, the more basic question of whether we should accept life as it comes arises. There's no easy yes or no to that.

But as people of faith we note that while Jesus' birth was not without planning, his life was without calculation.

THE EPIPHANY OF THE LORD

Readings: Isaiah 60:1-6; Ephesians 3:2-3, 5-6; Matthew 2:1-12

Upside Down

Nicknamed the 'green bomber,' a tiny worm that shoots out brilliant flares from its body in the presence of a predator has recently been discovered deep down in the Pacific Ocean. Less than 9 cm long, it adopts a strategy similar to that of a fighter pilot who uses flares as decoys against heat-seeking missiles. Faced with an enemy, this wily worm lets off bubbles of fluid that flare into flashes of light and glow brilliantly for several seconds to scare off predators.

Here we have a crafty use of light to keep undesirables away. In today's first reading we have light doing the opposite: bringing all types of people together. Light can attract or repel depending on what it reveals. Today's feast, The Epiphany of the Lord, reveals Christ manifesting himself to the Gentiles in the persons of the Magi.

The light of revelation in this event is a strange one. In story fashion it appears as a star that pinpoints the presence of the Christ for the Magi who were gentiles or non-Jews. When it finishes that job it turns to another: it shows the majesty of God's presence in the helplessness of a baby. Expecting to find the king of the Jews, the Magi find instead majesty in a manger. It must turn their expectations upside down.

The light of Christ must do the same for us: turn our expectations upside down. Are we brave enough to let it? Do we use our 'light' to show God's way to others, or like the worm, use it to repel 'undesirables'?

THE BAPTISM OF THE LORD

Readings: Isaiah 40:1-5, 9-11; Titus 2:11-14, 3, 4-7; Luke 3:15-16, 21-22

Renew not Recycle

According to one recycling agency, Ireland's consumption of alcohol over Christmas would fill '29 Olympic-sized swimming pools'. On average, adults drank 16 litres of alcohol or 2.5 times their own blood levels. If that's hard to swallow try this: the nation gobbled 4 million boxes of chocolates; guzzled 54 million cans and 15 million bottles of beer, 20 million bottles of wine, 4 million plastic bottles and 28 million cans of soft drinks. Households disposed of 96,500kg of packaging – equivalent to an adult's weight in cardboard per household – and 4 million sheets of gift-wrap paper. And that was in 2005! Just image what it must have been like every Christmas since then.

As Christmas celebrates Jesus' birth, how could recycling our waste produce seem more pressing a problem than renewing our faith in God and our service of each other? Our feasts are always occasions for renewal. Today's feast, the Baptism of the Lord, shows this. It reminds us of our own baptism and of what we are committed to because of it.

We need reminding from time to time that baptism, while it may have come easily, does not come cheaply. It does cost. Today's gospel reading makes that clear: 'He will baptise you with the Holy Spirit and fire.'

So, as we begin this New Year let us not take our baptism for granted, or forget it. That can so easily happen. When the Spirit's fire truly burns within us, we'll know that it's not for recycling used goods but for renewing God's gifts.

FIRST SUNDAY OF LENT

Readings: Deuteronomy 26:4-10; Romans 10:8-13; Luke 4:1-13

Morality Genes

After 20 years of research and God knows how much expense it's finally on the market: the blue rose. Not available in nature, it's the product of genetic manipulation. Someone, obviously not given to flowery language, has rather prosaically named it Applause. Marketed as a special occasion gift, for wedding anniversaries, birthdays and the likes, it retails at about €22 per stem. That should weed out the true romantics from the common or garden variety, don't you think?

What's that got to do with Lent? Nothing, really! I was just thinking that even with the impressive dedication and considerable resources that went into manufacturing this blushing freak of nature, you could wait until you were blue in the face before you'd see genetics modify a human being in to a better person. The day of the morality gene isn't just around the corner.

So, for those sensible enough to want to be a better person what more effective way to go about it than by listening to what Paul says in today's second reading: The word is near you, on your lips and in your heart. Lent is a time for listening. There's much sacrifice involved in listening well: sacrifice of time, emotional comfort and the luxury of aloofness. Is it going too far to say that those who don't listen to God's word can't listen to anyone else's?

What better way, then, to start Lent than by tuning in to God's word as we listen to our heart express its deepest desire. God's word, our heart? A rose by any other name …

SECOND SUNDAY OF LENT

Readings: Genesis 15:5-12, 17-18; Philippians 3:17-4:1; Luke 9:28-36

Identi-kit

If we regard all information gathered up to 1900 as one unit, since then that unit has doubled every ten years. We have shot dramatically from Stone Age to Information Age. But at heart we're still hunter-gatherers. Nowadays we 'hunt' for knowledge by gathering information. We've replaced spears with technology.

Take, for example, those wishing to establish paternity. A do-it-yourself DNA test-kit was due shortly in pharmacies across the UK in August 2009, according to one newspaper's report. Costing £29.99 with a £129 lab fee you would be able to establish paternity in less than five days.

If we read the Bible we can establish paternity in less than five minutes, and at no cost – financial, that is. But it's faith, not technology that recognises knowledge found in scripture as truth found in life. In today's second reading Paul speaks of our citizenship. He could just as easily speak of our paternity. He says: our citizenship is in heaven. We belong to another order of reality because that's the origin of our paternity. This is what the gospel reading is telling us too. A voice from the cloud addresses the transfigured Jesus as 'my Son', 'my Chosen'.

Being baptised in Jesus' name we share in his paternity, but by adoption. Jesus tells us to call God Father when we pray. So, as we pray this Lent, let's listen to our Father's word in scripture so that we accept ever more maturely and humbly a paternity that no identi-kit can establish – unless the D in DNA stands for 'divine'.

THIRD SUNDAY OF LENT

Readings: Exodus 3:1-8, 13-15; 1 Corinthians 10:1-6, 10-12; Luke 13:1-9

Googling is Good for You

A google a day keeps the doctor away, researchers have found. Surfing the Net, even more than reading, boosts the brain. And its effects last long after the surfing stops. One theory holds that surfing stretches the brain by making it perform multiple tasks simultaneously. Fine! But let's not forget what drives the search in the first place. And I don't mean the hard drive. I mean curiosity. Were this lacking there would be no activity. Curiosity stimulates the search.

It's what puts Moses in touch with God in our first reading today. He sees something that arouses his curiosity: a burning bush that's not consumed. His curiosity gets the better of him and because it does we discover two very important things – about God: he cares for us; about human beings: we're holy.

God tells Moses to come no closer and to take off his sandals because he's on holy ground – God's turf. I used to think that he was letting Moses know how unworthy he was to approach him. How wrong I was! God is saying the exact opposite. Not being gods we must maintain some distance from him, yet nothing should come between us, not even a pair of sandals. Only what comes directly from the hand of God is worthy to be near him – hence the naked sole.

Moses is a murderer. Yet God calls him. It's easy to see God through goodness. But can we see him when evil blocks the view? If not, then let's remember a murderer and a burning bush.

FOURTH SUNDAY OF LENT

Readings: Joshua 5:9-12; 1 Corinthians 5:17-21; Luke 15:1-3, 11-32

Computing Truth

The world's fastest computer makes 1,759 trillion calculations per second. Though faster than any human brain for calculating, it can't do the mundane problem-solving that Joe Soap does daily. Neither can it calculate what the important things in life are. Such things as meaning, purpose, destiny, friendship, service and love. Maybe that's because it doesn't have a mind of its own. But even humans with a mind of their own don't always calculate correctly either.

Take the prodigal son in today's gospel. He has a mind of his own, but focused on himself. If 'garbage in, garbage out' is the techno mantra for computers, then 'selfish in, selfish out' is the moral mantra for people. The father knows this, yet allows his son the freedom to act selfishly. Rather like God with us. If we don't use our head we'll suffer for it. Unfortunately, often so too will others. The father can object to his son's demand, but doesn't. He acknowledges that his son is a free agent. So he gets his way. Not surprisingly, it's the way to disaster. Back he comes to his father the wiser for a lesson that only life can teach him.

Wisdom doesn't come from machines, even from supercomputers that use 147,456 processors to simulate just 1 per cent of the human brain. The director of America's National Science Foundation claims that supercomputers 'let you get closer to the truth'. Good to know! Yet even better is to know that when you accept God's word without calculation you find real truth even more quickly.

FIFTH SUNDAY OF LENT

Readings: Isaiah 43:16-21; Philippians 3:8-14; John 8:1-11

Uprising

Somebody once said that just because he had 99 per cent of the DNA that Beethoven had that didn't make him a musician. Luckily, there's more to being human than DNA. Otherwise, we might be embarrassed by the fact that a worm, whose pet name is *C. Elegans,* shares up to 80 per cent of our genetic material. Next time you call someone a worm you might be more accurate than you think!

Some 4,000 of these low-life wigglers left their usual haunts of rubbish dumps and compost heaps in November 2009 for higher things – 322 kilometres higher to be exact. They became 'wormonauts' aboard the space shuttle Atlantis. Not in the least interested in being upwardly mobile, they went nevertheless on a 7-million kilometre journey so that scientists could study the effects of space travel on muscle-wastage.

Being upwardly mobile is what Paul yearns for in today's second reading but in a special way: the resurrection way. Paul yearns for something above and beyond his lot in life. And so he should. Genesis tells us imaginatively that we have come from the dust of the earth, not that we've been created to live in it. Our calling is to rise. Paul describes this as knowing the power of Christ's resurrection.

When evil tries to put us, and keep us, in the dirt we must not forget that we are called to higher things – not just 322 kilometres out in space, but throughout the vastness of eternity once we're transformed through dying. Want to worm your way out of that one?

PALM SUNDAY

Readings: Isaiah 50:4-7; Philippians 2:6-11; Luke 22:14-23:56

Online in Touch?

Who would think that the Internet is threatening the jury system! Well, it seems it is, according to England's most senior judge. The more people use the Internet, the fewer there are who get their information by listening. You go down the tubes and YouTube takes your place. So, sitting down for a long listen, concentrating on what's being said to evaluate its content may well become an art-form alien to a gadget-groping generation.

What, then, to make of today's first reading? 'The Lord has given me the tongue of a teacher … to sustain the weary with a word. Morning by morning he wakens my ear.' Use the Internet to get that sustaining word across? Well, it would get it *out* for sure, but *across* is another matter entirely. Getting something across means getting it in. It means entering someone's mind with a thought, a value, an understanding, perhaps even a vision and leaving it there. It means penetrating someone's heart to lay a gift of life-giving inspiration, of uplifting hope, of reassurance of one's worth before God, but above all to lay down his gift of shared love.

That's what a teacher's tongue can do, coming from the hand of God. That's what an ear can hear and a mind can comprehend when open to the Teacher's word. The question is: can that be done online? Should liturgy be in cyberspace, not sacred space? Would a virtual reality Palm Sunday skirt a real life Golgotha? The jury needn't be out too long on that.

EASTER SUNDAY

Readings: Acts 10:34, 37-43; Colossians 3:1-4; John 20:1-9

Surfing in the Highest

According to *The Times* newspaper (14/12/09) millions of young people in Britain are lonely despite having hundreds of so-called 'friends' on social networking sites. Presumably Britain is not alone in this. Those who seek friends at arms-length are bound to be unhappy. Friendship is intended to be right up close and personal. Virtual reality can't substitute for the real thing. Surfing the Net may seem cool, bright and breezy, even exciting; but it's well to remember that it's not called the 'net' for nothing. Being trapped by virtual friendships that may well be just illusionary, if not downright predatory, won't fill the void within an individual.

The survey of more than 2,000 adults found that loneliness was a major worry for 21 per cent of people aged 18-24, compared with only 8 per cent of those aged 55 and over.

Easter Sunday is the church's most important celebration. It may seem a bit of virtual reality to some, but not to those of faith. Jesus came right up close and personal to bring us resurrection. Today's second reading tells us what we should be 'surfing' for: the things that are above, where Christ is seated at the right hand of God. The 'catch', if you want to call it that, is that resurrection can't be found in virtual reality. You won't find it outside daily living with those you like and dislike.

Resurrection is rising through reality – even because of reality – to the glory God has in store for those who value real friends in real life.

SECOND SUNDAY OF EASTER

Readings: Acts 5:12-16; Apocalypse 1:9-13, 17-19; John 20:19-31

Gno your Genome

If you have $70,000 to spare you might want to buy the latest status symbol: a USB drive on a black velvet tray. But it's not any old finger file. It contains a digital version of your genome; sequenced, decoded and ready for use. So far, fewer than one hundred of the world's wealthiest individuals have succeeded in getting one.

There were only three personalised genomes on the planet in 2007. Since then the waiting list has increased steadily, world recession not withstanding. The urge to splurge springs not from scientific interest but from self-interest. The file's information may soon be able to tell its owner what he or she will die of. Consequently, they may be able to do something about it; thus thwarting the Grim Reaper's unwelcome embrace – at least for a time.

That's not the sort of healing we hear about, however, in today's first reading. It's completely unscientific and Spirit-driven. Significantly, it's more a case of seeking health than of thwarting death. As resurrection people we don't fear death, whatever about the business of dying. At least, we shouldn't. There is such a thing as a healthy acceptance of death, as there is an unhealthy fear of it.

Let's go further. For people of faith death is never followed by a full stop. In our thoughts, however, sometimes it is. That's why we need the Easter season – to remind us that death is not an ending of life but a beginning of resurrection. After all, we were born not for death but for eternal life.

THIRD SUNDAY OF EASTER

Readings: Acts 5:27-32, 40-41; Apocalypse 5:11-14; John 21:1-19

Jack-of-all-trades

Jack has been the most popular name for baby boys in Britain for 13 years running. In Ireland for a number of years it was the second most popular name to … yes, Seán. No playmate leapfrogging from John to Jack. It was up front, plain and simple, in-your-face-from-the-start, Jack. So what, you may ask. Well, it might indicate that the poetry of life has gone out the door for many parents and that a pedestrian prose has replaced it. If so, what a pity! With due apologies to the Jacks of all shades, the name does have its yawn factor.

The equally soporific Charles, on the other hand, can be an intoxicant when followed by the name Dickens for collectors of curios. Proof? Well, a 150-year-old wine bottle of his sold for £1,500. Just the bottle, empty! But then, it did have part of a label on the outside and dried sediment on the inside. But it was the owner's name that counted. Joe Blogg wouldn't have got a look in.

Today's first reading refers to a name: 'As they left the council they rejoiced that they were considered worthy to suffer dishonour for the sake of the name.' If a famous name can add so much value to an otherwise worthless object how much more so the name of Jesus when branded by baptism on a human heart! It's important that the 'brand' name 'Christian' be recognised through its bearer becoming 'all things to all men', and not just a Jack-of-all-trades to the few.

FOURTH SUNDAY OF EASTER

Readings: Acts 13:14, 43-52; Apocalypse 7:9, 14-17; John 10:27-30

Disarming

Things change during recession. People buy less and bargain-hunt more. They count their change. Supposedly, they go to church more often. Hard times, it seems, remind us of a soft God. A new one for me, however, is an increase in gun sales. American gunmaker Smith & Wesson is aiming for doubled annual sales for the next few years. After a 13 per cent hike in 2009, triggering sales to a whopping $335 million, they were expected to jump 30 per cent in the first quarter of this financial year – an impressive, or depressive depending on your viewpoint, $102 million increase.

Throughout the US demand for firearms is rising. The reason? Fear. Fear that recession-induced unemployment will lead to more crime. Fear that terrorism will again strike at the heartland. Fear that government will slap restrictions on gun ownership, and more taxes on firearms.

Today's gospel reading opens a fear-free zone. It radiates confidence. 'My sheep hear my voice. I know them, and they follow me. I give them eternal life, and they will never perish. No one will snatch them out of my hand.' This is not an arrogant boast but a sober statement of fact. The church knows she's awash with saints and sinners. Even when lifestyles and attitudes within the church betray the sorry fact of sin's influence on its members, the community's faith holds. The reason? Our God loves: in prosperity as well as in recession, and sinners as well as saints. Maybe sinners that little more, because they're short on love! Rather disarming, isn't it?

FIFTH SUNDAY OF EASTER

Readings: Acts 14:21-27; Apocalypse 21:1-5; John 13:31-35

Beauty and the Feast

Avatar is a visually stunning film. In 3-D the incredibly colourful and fantastic planet Pandora, where the story is fancifully set, totally captivates the imagination and sweeps one away on the light fantastic. Facing drab grey cement and noisy swarming traffic on leaving the cinema was also 'stunning' – but as in stunned, or dazed. The town where the cinema was set – also in 3-D – was anything but captivating by comparison. Indeed such comparison according to one newspaper report caused some people who had seen the film to experience bouts of depression afterwards. The comedown that real life is, was just too much for them. That report prodded me to see the film for myself. I'm glad I did. It reminded me never to underestimate the power of beauty to touch the human spirit, and to open up the human heart to the spiritual around, within and beyond us.

So let's open ourselves to the spiritual and mind-travel to that location of beauty in today's second reading: the new heaven and the new earth. We give our imagination free rein. We try to visualise the wonder of all things made new, glistening with health, spirit and immortality. We try to picture a level of life unlimited by anything, as we soar creatively achieving everything we were incapable of in this life. And that just for starters! Let's not be mean-minded or timid. The new heaven and the new earth leave fanciful Pandora in the shade and leave us to feast sumptuously in the radiant glory of God.

SIXTH SUNDAY OF EASTER

Readings: Acts 15:1-2, 22-29; Apocalypse 21:10-14, 22-23; John 14:23-29

Feeling like a Human Being

There's a memorable scene in *The Shawshank Redemption*. Andy Dufresne (Tim Robbins) plays *Duettino-Sull'aria* from Mozart's 'The Marriage of Figaro' over the prison loudspeaker system. Prisoners stop what they're doing enthralled by the operatic duet. As you watch their rapt features, 'Red' Redding's (Morgan Freeman) background commentary tells you that for a few minutes these prisoners feel like human beings again. The beauty of the music blocks out the ugliness of their surroundings and transports them to another place where refinement, beauty and spirit reign. It's a powerful, touching scene.

Now another scene. This time in Suffolk, England. A 5ft by 7ft dilapidated beach hut. Its window is broken. Its paint is peeling. It lacks a door, gas, electricity and water. A local council regulation forbids overnight use of it. For sale at a whopping £40,000, its estate agent says it'll be snapped up. Other huts similar in size but in better condition have sold even more 'whoppingly' for £100,000. Why? Location, location, location. They command a spectacular view of the sea. Again, a place of beauty – and for people of faith, a sense of Presence therein.

Our third and last scene is in today's second reading: the holy city Jerusalem coming down out of heaven from God. Refinement, beauty and Spirit reign there. No need for gas or electricity – not even for the Sun. The glory of God is its light, God's presence its air. Like the Shawshank prisoners we too need our moments of rapture whether it be from love, nature, art or faith. For without a peek into eternity, human nature just cannot peak.

SEVENTH SUNDAY OF EASTER

Readings: Acts of the Apostles 7:55-60; Apocalypse 22:12-14, 16-17, 20; John 17:20-26

What Money can't Buy

To be happy, be content with a salary of not more than €60,000. Earning more than that entails sacrifices that deaden the tingle of the jingle in your pocket: longer hours at work, shorter ones at home.

Two economists in Princeton University, New Jersey, conducted a poll of 450,000 Americans. Their findings were most interesting. Signs of happiness, viz. frequency of smiling and thinking positively, levelled off at the €60,000 pay grade. Smoking, obesity, divorce and headaches indicated unhappiness more than being poor did. And, you were more content if you were female, or religious or over 60. In particular, seeing life as having meaning and having a personal purpose in life greatly enhanced a person's emotional wellbeing, the study found.

Today's second reading has something to say about happiness too. It's teaching two things in particular. First, the Lord will soon return and reward us according to what we deserve. In other words, according to how we have fulfilled our purpose, or mission, in life. It reminds us that life has purpose and that it's short, even though we may act as if we're going to live forever. So, it's important to find out early in life what our personal mission is and start on it.

Second, the water of life – faith in Jesus as Saviour – is for all and it's free. That means that as we drink that water we open up to all people. And because the water is free we realise that happiness can't be bought for any price. So, why toil for more money than we need?

THE ASCENSION OF THE LORD

Readings: Acts 1:1-11; Ephesians 1:17-23; Luke 24:46-53

High-minded

A recent survey conducted by researchers at Durham University on people's attitude to sermons came up with some surprises: 96.6 per cent of those surveyed said they liked the Sunday sermon, and 60 per cent said it gave them a sense of God's love. Attitudes differed according to faith groupings. Evangelicals liked sermons most, Catholics wanted ones that educated rather than challenged. Baptists and Catholics favoured use of the Bible in sermons more than Anglicans and Methodists did. And, while Baptists wanted sermons to span an hour and then some, Catholics wanted them short. Ten minutes max.

So, what to say about the Ascension of the Lord that may be educative, and, yes, challenging too, yet brief? Its description in the first and third readings today takes only seconds to read. To focus the mind, then, let me ask you which you think is weirder: to believe that the Ascension was real, or to believe that a 6ft bronze sculpture by Alberto Giacometti, sold recently in Sotheby's, is really worth the £65 million paid for it.

The fact of the Ascension is of immeasurably more value than any worked-on piece of metal could possibly be. It has the power to stir the imagination, to engage the heart and to intrigue the mind with its promise. And, unlike artfully pressed and pounded metal, faith in the Ascension has the power to effect change. Belief in God's Word ascending can raise even hearts of stone with money to burn, to hearts of flesh burning with love for those who suffer.

PENTECOST SUNDAY

Readings: Acts 2:1-11; Romans 8:8-17; John 14:15-16, 23-26

Reachers not Preachers

Where would we be without scientists? Certainly not in the calmest place on earth. For it is they who have pinpointed just that place. The mother of all 'getaways' you might think, but don't make plans to go there just yet. Problem is it's not a gorgeous tropical island but an icy plateau in Antarctica. Situated several hundred miles from the South Pole this place, sporting the alluring name of Ridge A, has an atmosphere so still that stars don't twinkle there. Its air is 100 times drier than the Sahara's. And its average winter temperature of -70°C makes it the coldest place on earth too.

But when we're looking for a calm refuge from life's stress and strain we don't have to budge from where we are. We find peace and calm in our hearts, or we don't find it at all. One of the surest things to disturb one's peace of mind is a relationship gone sour. One where communication has ceased. Communicating well calms the heart. It's interesting that the first effect of God's Spirit coming upon the apostles is their new ability to communicate without barriers to all and sundry.

In less dramatic fashion that's true today too. Nobody has much difficulty with understanding the language of goodness, kindness and love. A smile says the same thing in any language. It doesn't need translation. Neither does a helping hand. It's not preachers that we need today to spread God's word but 'reachers' – people who reach out to others be they Parthians, Medes, or Elamites – or their modern-day equivalents.

THE MOST HOLY TRINITY

Readings: Proverbs 8:22-31; Romans 5:1-5; John 16:12-15

God is ...?

Clue: Mexican salamander. Seven letters. What is it? Haven't a clue? Starts with a and ends in l. No? Middle letter is l. So it has to be ... axolotl. Ah! The stuff of addictions. The first newspaper crossword puzzle appeared in the *New York World*, 1913. Englishman, Arthur Wynne, its creator called it a word-cross. Ten years on it had soared to the status of a national craze. Even then some media people decried it as a national threat because of the hours 'squandered' on it by all and sundry alike.

Today, Trinity Sunday, we don't celebrate a puzzle, but we do pay homage to a mystery. Puzzles get solved, mysteries don't. They're not for solving. The more you delve into a mystery the more you realise there is to delve into. Thus it is with that mystery we so abstractedly call the Most Holy Trinity.

God is not an abstraction. God is person. Three in fact. Though no less mysterious for it, God is more accessible to our minds and hearts by being seen as Father, Son and the Spirit of love between them. God is not a cold, unfeeling, unit of isolated magnificence. He is the father running out to welcome home a repentant brat of a son. He is the Son who couldn't resist becoming one of us even though he would have to pay the ultimate price for doing so. And, unlike pagan gods to be feared, God is Spirit inspiring love in the hearts of all people of good will.

Clue: God. Four letters. Solution?

THE BODY AND BLOOD OF CHRIST

Readings: Genesis 14:18-20; 1 Corinthians 11:23-26; Luke 9:11-17

Imagine that!

Brainstorming is about to take on new meaning if research in brain science has its way. Already scientists can convert into crude video footage the brain's activity from watching or even remembering something. In the US security agencies are experimenting with brain scanners for interrogating prisoners. They're also studying ways of scanning brains from a distance to probe a person's thoughts and anxieties without their knowledge, for example at airports.

The Eucharist also probes – but the heart, and up close and personal – to share thoughts, feelings and anxieties. It doesn't intrude into your privacy but invites you to a faith-filled encounter with God and friends. It eases life's burdens through mutual support, affirmation and service. It does so through sharing time, talents and goodwill with others, not just during Mass but also outside of it.

We see this in today's gospel reading. Jesus tells his disciples to feed the crowd following him. They say they don't have enough food to go round. That doesn't bother Jesus. So they just do what they're told and start sharing the little they have. And, surprise, surprise, they have more than enough to feed everybody. This is why Jesus gave us the Eucharist. This is why we go to Mass. To become sharers with others. To give to, and accept from, another human being.

I wonder if our brains were scanned as we celebrate the Eucharist what images would be reproduced: those of daze, flatlined by consubstantiality, or those of vision pulsating from simple words of life?

SECOND SUNDAY IN ORDINARY TIME

Readings: Isaiah 62:1-5; 1 Corinthians 12:4-11; John 2:1-11

Seeing Red

I wonder if the UK-chart-topping, 1986 hit 'Lady in Red' by Chris de Burgh would have soared so high had she been in green. Wearing red not only gets you noticed, it can get you ahead even in the Olympic Games, according to one lecturer at Durham University, England. Wearing red marks you as aggressive and dominant.

Today's second reading lists distinguishing marks for members of the Christian community. The colour red doesn't get a look in. Neither does designer labels, gym workouts, health-food diets, or high-tech gizmos (even had they existed). But then they wouldn't; all the qualities listed are for service, not dominance, or ego-gratification. Also, everything on the list is internal to the individual, not external. I don't need to enhance my appearance for service, but I do need to enhance my self. And the gifts listed in this reading do just that: wise utterance, knowledgeable speech, faith witness, power to heal, working miracles, prophesying, the ability to discern spirits, talking in tongues and interpreting them.

To put these gifts in more contemporary wrapping we might list them as: having cop on, being informed, practising what I preach, comforting those in difficulty, helping without counting the cost, being my brother's keeper, being in touch with life's basics, being open to God's Spirit and open to those open to God's Spirit.

It's surprising at times that were you to go public, so to speak, and say that these are the qualities that distinguish true Christians some of that public, even those not Christian, would probably see red!

THIRD SUNDAY IN ORDINARY TIME

Readings: Nehemiah 8:2-6, 8-10; 1 Corinthians 12:12-30; Luke 1:1-4, 4:14-21

Your Bottom Dollar

Gambling is one of our growing problems. You can bet your bottom dollar on that! It's estimated that in 2008 punters risked losing about €3.6 billion in the nation's 1,093 betting shops. That's €300 million more than the previous year. No recession there! This, alarmingly, doesn't include on-course betting, gambling on the National Lottery, or online. Many people relish risk, crave for chance, and feed on fickle fate instead of solid faith. For some people there can be nothing odd with the odds when it comes to risk-taking for money. What, in sober moments, most of us would count as throwing money away, gung-ho gamblers see as a prelude to a victory parade.

Today's gospel reading doesn't deal with chance, though there may be some risk later down the road. It presents us with odds-on certainty: the fulfilment of the prophecy of Isaiah in the person of Jesus. He was prophesied as the one who brings news of freedom to captives and those oppressed because the Spirit of God rests on him. In other words, because God is with Jesus he can enable us to live free of addictions, compulsions, and false values. It's a totally upbeat prophecy, and indeed Jesus is totally upbeat about it. Question is: are we?

Do we accept Jesus as he who brings us freedom? Or, do we see him as cramping our style? But there's nothing that's moral and legal that we can't do as a Christian that we could do were we not. You can bet your bottom dollar on that too.

FOURTH SUNDAY IN ORDINARY TIME

Readings: Jeremiah 1:4-5, 17-19; 1 Corinthians 12:31-13:13; Luke 4:21-30

Climate Change

There's something fishy about the North Sea. It's getting hotter. Its temperature rose by 1°C over the last 40 years. Not earth shaking, but serious enough to cause waves. The plankton that cod larvae like have had it. Some 60 per cent of them have scuttled off to a cooler clime 1,200km further north. The result? A sea change. Cod stocks dwindled; crabs stocks exploded and jellyfish proliferated as the adult cod that feed on these became fewer. This in turn put pressure on flatfish such as plaice and sole whose offspring crabs crave. Just one extra degree of heat and an ecosystem's food chain snaps. Even the quiet, away-from-it-all sea urchins, mussels and scallops on the seabed haven't escaped the squeeze.

Now, let's enter our fishbowl and look at our society, our North Sea. Even here, one little degree of change can produce unforeseen consequences. I still remember the shock nearly 30 years ago while home on holidays from the missions hearing a seven-year old girl shout at a five-year-old boy and call him an a**hole. I thought only foul-mouthed Hollywood hoodlums used that language. I figured she'd been exposed at home to so-called entertainment unsuited even to adults. I fume when I hear on the TV seemingly concerned warnings from a disembodied voice about a film containing what it arbitrarily calls 'strong' language. It's never 'foul' or 'bad', always 'strong'. What a fine positive and 'adult' term for something that's debasing!

Needless to say, a lot more has entered the fishbowl from Hollywood and elsewhere that has raised the temperature.

FIFTH SUNDAY IN ORDINARY TIME

Readings: Isaiah 6:1-8; 1 Corinthians 15:1-11; Luke 5:1-11

In the Dark

When it comes to energy and matter we're in the dark. Satellite images of leftover energy from the Big Bang show things as they were 400,000 years after the Bang. To put that into perspective: it means seeing something as it was 13 billion years ago. Analysing their findings, scientists have discovered that only 4.6 per cent of the total universe is made of stuff we can see. The rest, in the form of dark matter and dark energy, is invisible and mystifying. Dark matter holds our galaxies together; dark energy drives them apart. Their interaction means that while there won't be more matter in the universe there will be more space – lots more. So much more that neighbouring galaxies will disappear into the void. We'll find ourselves even more cosmically isolated than we already are. Something to look forward to!

Better to look forward to what God's word promises. God's image in today's first reading shows him as majestic and transcendent. Yet he cares for his people. He sends Isaiah on a mission to them. This mighty God, for whom our Big Bang was neither big nor a bang, cares for his creation. A cold and lonely universe is not part of his plan for us.

Couldn't be since he sends his son to us later. As the seraphs cover their faces before the majesty of God in that first reading, so too does Peter as he falls before Jesus' knees in awe in the gospel reading.

Take your pick: dark matter, dark future; glorious God, glorious future.

SIXTH SUNDAY IN ORDINARY TIME

Readings: Jeremiah 17:5-8; 1 Corinthians 15:12, 16-20; Luke 6:17, 20-26

Grand Finale

The Hubble Space Telescope has shown the universe in such incredible detail that it has transformed the way scientists view it. For example, Hubble has honed down the estimate of the universe's age to between 13 and 14 billion years. It was instrumental in discovering dark energy – that mysterious force that accelerates the expansion of the universe. And, it has revealed galaxies at all stages of their evolution: from wobbly toddlers to the end-time collapse of their massive stars. Among the world's most important observatories ever, Hubble will degrade until it can't function. Its life expectancy is relatively short. However, the rejuvenation it got in May 2009 from the crew of the space shuttle Atlantis will enable it to go out in a blaze of glory. Hubble's last years will be its best.

The same often holds true for people. Senior ones, when they've lived good lives, have so much to offer. We should never be tempted to think that we're passed it, or have become useless. The doing may be less urgent, varied or demanding, but the being becomes more important than ever. The older we are privileged to get, when open to God's Spirit, the more we give witness to the truth of what Paul writes about in today's second reading. We are called to resurrection – a resurrection that begins today, or for the fortunate ones yesterday.

As Hubble has revolutionised scientists' view of the universe, so too can every person whose resurrection has begun revolutionise the outlook and behaviour of those still awaiting theirs.

SEVENTH SUNDAY IN ORDINARY TIME

Readings: 1 Samuel 26:2, 7-9, 12-13, 22-23; 1 Corinthians 15;45-49; Luke 6:27-38

One up for Put-downs

One-liners can be deadly. Recently while talking with a friend we got round to the matter of put-downs. He told me of one he'd received not so long ago. While at a party, he was talking to a friend called John less than graciously about a mutual acquaintance of theirs called Stephen. John, a good listener, let him go on and on. Then when he had finished his character assassination of the hapless Stephen, John just said quite disarmingly 'Oh, I'm surprised to hear you say that about Stephen. He always speaks so well of you.'

Tongue-control doesn't come easily. But today's gospel reading shows how essential it is that we have it. Jesus tells us to bless and pray for those who curse us and treat us badly. In other words, we must speak well of them. To help us do so a broad perspective is necessary.

Jesus, here, is talking about wide-ranging compassion, not just about speaking well of others. What he's calling for is the practice of goodwill towards all people, at all times, including any we might regard as enemy.

The standards he set are high, very high indeed. To reach them a shift in mindset is called for. The need for that shift has a very long history, going right back in fact to the first one-liner ever used in the Bible: Cain's cheeky comment to God: 'Am I my brother's keeper?' God was not put-down. But Cain was certainly put out. He became a wanderer, marked for life.

Like compassion, evil can be wide-ranging too.

EIGHTH SUNDAY IN ORDINARY TIME

Readings: Sirach 27:4-7; 1 Corinthians 15:54-58; Luke 6:39-45

Brain-game

Some so-called brain-training software packages have sold over 35 million copies. Companies that produce them are brain-trained enough not to claim that they are scientifically proven to improve ability to acquire knowledge and understanding. Brain-training games are now a billion-dollar business. So there must be some smart brains at play somewhere. Surprisingly then, a combined University of Cambridge and BBC study showed that in intelligence tests the most consistent users of brain-training games performed no better than equally committed internet surfers.

Today's first reading and gospel would seem to imply the need for some kind of brain-training – but not the type on offer from computer games. It's more a question of acquiring what today we call 'cop on,' or of learning to apply common sense to life. 'Do not praise a man before he has spoken, since this is the test of men,' Sirach advises. Sound advice, indeed! 'Take the plank out of your own eye first, and then you will see clearly enough to take out the splinter that is in your brother's eye,' Jesus tells us.

We're never short of sound advice – only receptive ears to take it in. But even when we do listen and try to put into practice what we hear, there's no guarantee of success. We may change for a time but so often slip back into old habits.

When it comes to talk, care is called for. I doubt if any software could train our brains to prize discretion and integrity; respect truth and honesty and avoid hypocrisy. But if there were, I'd be game to play.

NINTH SUNDAY IN ORDINARY TIME

Readings: 1 Kings 8:41-43; Galatians 1:1-2, 6-10; Luke 7:1-10

Away with Words

Texting is causing problems for teenagers. Their mobiles are miring them in verbal mediocrity. Generally speaking, most teenagers have a 40,000-word vocabulary by the age of 16. But to speed things up kids who text each other abbreviate awesomely and limit their vocabulary to about 800 words, according to one expert. They'll find out that they need more than that to get a job.

A linguistics professor at Lancaster University analysed some 10m words of written down teenspeak, and 100,000 words found on teenagers' blogs. The twenty most used words, including 'yeah', 'no' and 'but', made up about one third of all words used. That might be okay for cool chat on trendy topics, but not for communicating with the rest of the planet. A British government adviser on communications recommends no more than half an hour's daily TV viewing for tots under two. Anything more hampers conversation with real people.

The elders in today's gospel reading, who plead with Jesus on behalf of the centurion, have no problems with conversation. So persuasive are they that Jesus goes with them to the centurion's house. And so articulate is the centurion in expressing his faith that Jesus cures his sick servant.

Being able to express oneself clearly and fluently is very important. It contributes to a healthy self-image and boosts self-confidence. And it comes in handy when you want to achieve something in life, especially if that's spreading God's word. You can't text God's word into the human heart. Even Facebook has little to offer here. It's the face-to-face approach that counts.

TENTH SUNDAY IN ORDINARY TIME

Readings: 1 Kings 17:17-24; Galatians 1:11-19; Luke 7:11-17

Voice Recognition

There are over 6,000 languages spoken in the world today. Imagine what it would be like to know all of them. Soon any such aspiration may become redundant. Google is working on software for phones to translate foreign languages almost instantly. Already it has an automatic system that can translate text in 52 languages on computers. It also operates a voice recognition system that allows phone users to surf the Net by speaking commands instead of typing them. But the really big hurdle remains: regional accents. No system for voice recognition can deal with those yet.

Voice recognition was not a problem for St Paul. In today's second reading he confidently claims that God called him through his grace and chose to reveal his Son in him. That's quite a claim. Yet there's no doubt in Paul's mind about this. God chose him, he tells us, to preach the good news about Jesus to the pagans. Again, no doubt.

Looking at this with the eyes of faith, it's not surprising. When God communicates with somebody they'll know it. Otherwise, his word would be frustrated. And we know from the Old Testament (Is 55:11) that God's word never returns to him empty but succeeds in the thing for which he sends it. So clear is it when God communicates that there is no need to consult with anyone about it. In Paul's case, he just ups and goes.

God communicates with us too from time to time. When we're attuned to his word we won't need voice recognition aids. Like Paul, we'll know. The question is, will we up and go?

ELEVENTH SUNDAY IN ORDINARY TIME

Readings: 2 Samuel 12:7-10, 13; Galatians 2:16, 19-21; Luke 7:36-8:3

Soft Touch

A gribble is a sea worm, 1-4 mm long, and a pest. The scourge of seafarers, gribbles bore into ships' planks and wreck them. Digesting their cellulose, they cause much destruction to marine timber structures such as jetties and piers. But, they're peerless when it comes to recycling driftwood. Researchers have found that the enzymes gribbles use to break down woody cellulose and turn it into energy-rich sugars could convert wood and straw to liquid biofuel. So today's pest may become tomorrow's pet. By doing a-what-comes-naturally they help the environment.

The woman in today's gospel reading is also doing a-what-comes-naturally. While it seems outrageous to the Pharisee that Jesus should be at ease with a woman of her type touching him, it really is a case of both her and Jesus doing a-what-comes-naturally: she, a sinner approaching him for forgiveness, and he, the Saviour, accepting the sinner graciously. The only one feeling discomfort is the Pharisee on the sideline. Despite any appearance to the contrary, that can prove an uncomfortable place to be, at least for Christians, the self-righteous and hypocrites.

Jesus is open to all people, particularly those whom society is closed to. But he's more than open. He doesn't wait in the wings for them to approach him. He seeks them out and brings them centre stage.

Just as researchers have discovered that the grubby little gribble has something worthwhile to offer society, so too do we discover that those whom society considers grubby have much to offer when we regard them as Jesus does.

TWELFTH SUNDAY IN ORDINARY TIME

Readings: Zechariah 12:10-11, 13:1; Galatians 3:26-29; Luke 9:18-24

Crying Shame

It's official: women cry more than men do. Researchers in Germany have discovered that while men shed tears six to 17 times a year, women do so 30 to 64 times. And, whereas men go with the flow for two to four minutes, women's tear ducts, once activated, stay in hyperdrive for up to six minutes. Furthermore, if a woman starts weeping she accelerates to full-blown sobbing in 65 per cent of cases. For men, it's six per cent. Now to end this mini-deluge of drippy data: women cry when they feel inadequate, face dicey situations, or when remembering past events; men cry from empathy, or because of a failed relationship.

That last bit makes me wonder how Peter feels in today's gospel reading when Jesus practically rebukes him for giving an honest answer to his question. Jesus is praying; stops for a moment, and as if still in prayer asks a worried question: Who do people say I am? He doesn't react when his disciples say John the Baptist, or Elijah, or a prophet, but he comes down heavily on them when Peter nails him as the Messiah. This is too close to the bone. Jesus' hour for self-acceptance has not yet come. But it will. He journeys to self-knowledge and self-acceptance as we do: gradually.

On that same journey our personal question is not about what others think of me but about what I think of myself. Has my 'hour' come for my discovery and acceptance of self as God's son or daughter? If not, what a crying shame!

THIRTEENTH SUNDAY IN ORDINARY TIME

Readings: 1 Kings 19:16, 19-21; Galatians 5:1, 13-18; Luke 9:51-62

Testy Times

It used to be the terrible teens. Now it's the terrible tots. Crèches in Britain are suspending up to 14 young children a day, aged five and younger, for physical assault. Incidents where testy tots use violence against classmates and teachers rose six per cent in a year.

I wonder what sort of tots the two disciples were in today's gospel reading. If they weren't testy as tots they're certainly testy as adults. Inflated with importance they assume a power to 'command fire to come down from heaven' and torch to death the inhabitants of a Samaritan village. Not very Christian that, now is it?

Though close to Jesus physically as his followers, they aren't yet close enough to him spiritually to recognise what sort of person and what sort of messiah he is. It seems there's baggage blocking the way: religious baggage that inflates their sense of election, of being God's own people to the exclusion of others; political baggage that expects a freedom-fighter messiah to liberate the Jews from Roman tyranny; and social baggage that cultivates an elitist mentality that seduces them into thinking they can ride rough-shod over people like the Samaritans whom they despise.

Some ancient authorities add, 'as Elijah did' to v 54 about commanding fire from heaven. In response to this hankering for former ways and attitudes, Jesus rebukes them. I wonder does he have any such rebuke for us today as we carry our baggage, whether it be personal, social or institutional in these testy and testing times?

FOURTEENTH SUNDAY IN ORDINARY TIME

Readings: Isaiah 66:10-14; Galatians 6:14-18; Luke 10:1-12, 17-20

Cross Purpose

Parents can be pushy, a study has found. Not satisfied with their kids' long school day, many parents muscle their munchkins into an assortment of after-school activities. Counting the hours of a regular school day, of heaped homework, of club commitments and of pursuing hobbies shows that children can average up to 53 hours of work a week. And all in the name of achievement!

Well, for Paul in today's second reading nothing short of becoming a new creation fits the bill for achievement. As he says, 'a new creation is everything'. However, his formula for success is not the No 1 of most people. His is an attitude of boasting of nothing other than the cross of Jesus Christ.

Does he mean that physical, cross-beamed implement of torture used to kill him? Let's hope not. The cross as a piece of wood has no special significance. What is significant is Jesus' loving faithfulness to his Father, and his integrity in witnessing to what he believed in, that enabled him to face the horror of the cross. This same love of God and uncompromising commitment to his mission is what fastens Paul to the world and the world to him.

Far from being a catalyst for depression, or the trigger for a spirituality of gloom, the cross – though stark and uncompromising – nevertheless reveals a heart warm with love for God and his creation. Our 'cross' will weigh us down if borne with gripe, but will raise us up if borne with grace.

FIFTEENTH SUNDAY IN ORDINARY TIME

Readings: Deuteronomy 30:10-14; Colossians 1:15-20; Luke 10:25-37

On the Run

If you run, take note. Running barefoot is best. Results from a Harvard University study show that people are born to run without shoes. For two million years we ran barefoot, landing untutored, on the sides or balls of our feet thus letting our heels down lightly. However, since the 1970s when running shoes took off we have begun to develop a new gait. Now comfortably shod, we land heavily on our heels with every stride we take – with about three times the impact of barefoot running. This increases the likelihood of suffering stress-related injuries. So if you don't want to put your foot in it, go *au naturel*.

Today's first reading and the gospel are about doing-a-what-comes-naturally. The first reading tells us that it's easy to find God's word. It's in our mouth and in our heart. Could anything be more natural than to listen to what's so close to us?

The gospel describes the coldness of two types of law-observant people: a priest and a Levite. Both served the great symbol of established Judaism: the Temple, one in liturgy, the other in administration. Both feared contamination from a seemingly dead person. Both obeyed the rules – but betrayed their humanity. Both sacrificed the greater good for the lesser. Both put symbol before substance: the symbol of God's presence in stone before the reality of that presence in flesh.

They ran their race wrongly. They ran *from* because of law instead of running *to* because of compassion. Well shod, no doubt, they didn't run barefoot.

SIXTEENTH SUNDAY IN ORDINARY TIME

Readings: Genesis 18:1-10; Colossians 1:24-28; Luke 10:38-42

Clutter

Laptops are turning lecture halls into private cinemas and even online casinos. Once considered valuable aides to learning, they're no longer the apple of a teacher's eye. An increasing number of lecturers just don't want them in the classroom anymore. The reason? Students use them less for learning and more for entertaining. Themselves, that is. Not only are those who use them distracted, but so too are those nearby them. Not surprising when laptop use in class becomes networking in Facebook, watching movies, waging World War III virtually and playing poker actually, online. Instead of focusing on teacher talking, students focus on their laptop calling. So, the teacher strikes back, banning them from the classroom. This is a clear example of how something good, the amazing laptop, can get in the way of something better, the desired education.

Today's gospel reading gives another example of the same thing. Jesus visits Martha and Mary. The good here – Martha's attention to guests – gets in the way of something better: her attention to God's word. Mary, on the other hand, just sits absorbed by what Jesus is saying. She's free of clutter in her life and so can focus on what's important. Activity is fine, but it shouldn't push contemplation from our lives.

A Buddhist monk once told Thomas Merton, a famous American Trappist, that you can't contemplate properly until you can close doors quietly. Closing doors quietly on clutter – mental, emotional and social – is what today's gospel is about. You may lap that up, but you won't top it!

SEVENTEENTH SUNDAY IN ORDINARY TIME

Readings: Genesis 18:20-32; Colossians 2:12-14; Luke 11:1-13

Hardwired for God

I don't know if our genes are, but according to scientists our brains are: hardwired for God. They're programmed to discover supernatural reasons for life's mysteries. Our brain organises the information our senses send it to discover cause and effect. Since babies only12-months old can do this, it seems to be innate rather than acquired. So, the findings of researchers at Bristol University studying the development and workings of children's brains are not surprising. They indicate that belief systems offer a possible evolutionary benefit to people.

An itch to ask the question 'why' is not the only thing that's innate to us. There's the universal hope, expectation even, that good will conquer evil. Just read your novels, watch your films. Don't you feel more satisfied when the good guy wins? Even books and films with ambiguous endings aren't as emotionally satisfying as those with a clear-cut victory where the one who is good wins out against all the odds. That feel-good factor when good conquers all comes with the job, so to speak, of being human.

It's this faith in goodness, more specifically in God, that's the basis for what today's gospel reading tells us: 'Ask, and it will be given you; search and you will find …' Scripture is telling us that God doesn't take us for a ride. He's not a messer, if you'll pardon the slang. He's consistent and we can trust him.

That's the God we're hardwired to believe in, the one who gives the Holy Spirit to those who ask him.

EIGHTEENTH SUNDAY IN ORDINARY TIME

Readings: Ecclesiastes 1:2, 2:21-23; Colossians 3:1-5, 9-11; Luke 12:13-21

Vanity of Vanities

Brain scans are revealing. Take the ones done on teenagers listening to music. These show that insecurity and not personal preference dictates what songs they call 'cool'. In one study they listened to tracks and rated how much they liked them. After a break, they listened to them again some having been shown a popularity rating based on how many times a track had been downloaded. While 12 per cent of those who didn't know whether others liked a track or not changed their ratings, 22 per cent of those who knew that a tune was a hit changed theirs. Of those, three quarters moved in tune with the song's popularity rating.

Now for the interesting bit: the first time they heard a track their reward and pleasure zones lit up; but on listening again their anxiety and pain centres glowed. This suggested that fear made them change their views.

Today's first reading is tailor-made for that sort of thing. 'Vanity of vanities!' it proclaims, 'All is vanity.' It sees human toil as an annoyance, and notes that even at night our minds don't rest. Worry persists. We don't like truth packaged in pessimism. Yet, truth made one researcher remark that many people who think they're individuals with free choice actually are slaves to what others think.

Those words on vanity from the 3rd century BC could just as easily be from today, so accurately do they hit the spot. If we have to be slaves to what another thinks, then let that other be the Other.

NINETEENTH SUNDAY IN ORDINARY TIME

Readings: Wisdom 18:6-9; Hebrews 11:1-2, 8-19; Luke 12:32-48

On the Ball

Scientists can be on the ball just as much as footballers. Take Danish physicist Niels Bohr (d. 1962) for example. He watched westerns. As he did, he noted that something strange happened in them: the gunslinger who went for his gun first, often was the one who was shot first – even though he had the advantage. Bohr was fast enough to draw the correct conclusion from what he saw: reacting is faster than acting. It has now been confirmed that we move faster when we react to something that some else is doing than when we start to do something ourselves – about 21 milliseconds faster.

How fast are we on the draw when responding to God's word? In today's gospel reading God says he gives us the kingdom. How do we react to that? Do we change because of it? God doesn't hesitate to give. We mustn't hesitate to respond. We can't claim that we don't know what to do because it's spelled out for us: we've to sell our possessions, give alms, make purses that don't wear out because the treasure they contain is in heaven; we've to be dressed for action, have our lamps lit and be ready for the Master's return. In short, we react to the gift of God's kingdom by living like people who belong to it. So we live with thanks for the precious gift of life. We share that gift graciously with others. We react to life with love, generosity, faith and courage.

That's really being on the ball!

TWENTIETH SUNDAY IN ORDINARY TIME

Readings: Jeremiah 38:4-6, 8-10; Hebrews 12:1-4; Luke 12:49-53

Kick-start Coffee Gets the Boot

'I never take coffee in the morning. It keeps me awake all day,' one wag quipped. He'd be surprised by the findings of a study at the University of Bristol. Researchers tested 379 individuals to find out just how perky coffee made them. The participants stayed off caffeine for 16 hours. Then they were given either caffeine in pill form, or a placebo. Computer tests followed to assess their alertness. Surprisingly, these showed little difference between those who swallowed caffeine pills or placebos. Researchers concluded that coffee's coveted kick to start the day rolling might be an illusion. As regular coffee drinkers develop a tolerance for caffeine, its kick doesn't send them high but merely to their normal level of performance by easing caffeine-withdrawal symptoms.

How many people of faith, I wonder, try the word of God to get the day off to a good start. Instead of gulping down coffee how many arrange their life in such a way that they can take five – with their bible and let one thought grip them and guide them for the day. Take for example, today's second reading. Take a thought from that. It tells us to throw off everything that hinders our running steadily in the race we have started – and it's not the race to the office!

It's the race that leads us to God, fuelled by the words and power of Jesus to keep us on track. Caffeine kicks may be an illusion; God's words are not. Unlike coffee they won't keep us awake all day, but they will waken us up to the blessing that is each and every day.

TWENTY-FIRST SUNDAY IN ORDINARY TIME

Readings: Isaiah 66:18-21; Hebrews 12:5-7, 11-13; Luke 13:22-30

The Punisher

An atheist doesn't usually feel the need for a supernatural being – and one that's a punisher to boot! But at the 2009 annual conference of the British Association of Science, its president said that religion may have helped to protect society from itself in the past, and may be needed to do so again. His concern was not for divinity but for human failure, as he saw it, to take effective action against global warming. A supernatural punisher, he suggested, might be part of the solution. That's raising global warming to the fire and brimstone temperature of pulpit thumpers of yesteryear!

He'd like today's second reading as it talks about being punished by the Lord. However, verse 6 is a quotation from the Book of Proverbs 3:12. The language there is softer, less punitive than in Hebrews, at least in the NRSV Bible. In Proverbs we have 'reprove' not 'punish', and a father who 'delights' in his son, and not merely 'accepts' him, as in Hebrews.

Impressions are important. They must never blur our image of the loving God we believe in. He who delights in us is not vindictive or judgemental. But neither is he a softie. Evil exists up to its most abhorrent forms because of a misuse of the freedom our loving God gave us. When we misuse it there are consequences always. They're built in to the way things are. Unfortunately, there are times when we can't seem to learn by any other means than through the dire consequences of our acts.

TWENTY-SECOND SUNDAY IN ORDINARY TIME

Readings: Sirach 3:17-20, 28-29; Hebrews 12:18-19, 22-24; Luke 14:1, 7-14

High Flyers

Cleo, a 13-year-old pet parrot, is usually a model macaw. But one day she had a panic attack and just lost it. She shot up 15m (50ft) into a tree and couldn't come down. Having branched out, she fazed out. Her owner had to hire a cherry picker to bring the petrified parrot down to earth. Cleo had never flown so high before, her owner said, and she thought that the unfortunate bird just didn't know how to come down. The moral of the story? Don't be a bird-brained high flyer.

Today's readings have high flyers and 'bird brains' in mind when they say: be humble. Sirach tells us to go about our business with humility. Luke gives some street-wise advice on not being pushy in public and hogging the limelight. Both readings come with a health warning on losing the run of ourselves.

Humility gets a bad press usually. It seems a weakness to many, a sign of immaturity, or a personality defect. Today's go-getter *geist* is aggressive and competitive, not kind and co-operative. It operates an in-your-face, nothing-succeeds-like-success marketplace. There are no humility-friendly zones there.

In part, that's because humility isn't a loner. It brings friends: reverence for the sacredness of human life, respect for every person, a willingness to accept gracefully that others may be more intelligent, gifted and capable. And the most bothersome buddy of all: regard for God.

To prevent panic attacks, and high flying that puts you out on a limb, avoid cherry picking. Just take the straight and narrow.

TWENTY-THIRD SUNDAY IN ORDINARY TIME

Readings: Wisdom 9:13-18; Philemon 9-10,12-17; Luke 14:25-33

Whole-hearted

You hear them in the street, on buses and on trains: mobile phone conversations. They can be annoying, for two reasons at least. First, some users of phones seem to think it necessary to shout into them presumably because of the distance between themselves and those at the other end. Second, you get only a 'halfalogue' – one side of the conversation.

Scientists at Cornell University, New York, claim that hearing only one half of a conversation is more draining on one's attention than hearing all of it. They experimented with students who were given concentration exercises while hearing one or two speakers on mobile phones. Their conclusion: people are less able to divert their attention from a half-heard conversation than from a fully heard one.

Half of anything rarely satisfies. It can even be irksome. It's the whole hog or nothing. The same can be said for half-hearted effort.

Take today's gospel reading for example. It ends on a note that could be sombre, or joyful, depending on the generosity of one's response to it: 'None of you can become my disciple if you do not give up all your possessions.' What a prospect! You can't follow Jesus half-heartedly. It's total commitment, or no commitment. To put flesh on that, it means there can be no Jesus-free zones in my life; that nothing in life is more important than the values he holds out to me. Therefore, I don't sacrifice these, ever, for anything else.

I wonder how many of us get that part of the conversation?

TWENTY-FOURTH SUNDAY IN ORDINARY TIME

Readings: Exodus 32:7-11, 13-14; 1 Timothy 1:12-17; Luke 15:1-32

'Tea-ing' off

You've heard of black tea, green tea, herbal tea, and high tea. Well now there's philosophical tea. A new fad is sweeping *La France*. There, children as young as eight are acquiring a taste for philosophical tea. Difficult though it may be to swallow at this remove, nevertheless, many parents in France want their children to cut their metaphysical 'munchers' on heavy issues over light refreshments. Children, they believe, should be encouraged to debate life's mysteries from the time they discover the words 'what' and 'why' to give them an early handle on a complex world.

The tea parties are held in cafés, public libraries and homes. Cakes and fruit juices feature prominently to sweeten debates drizzled with Descartes, sprinkled with Socrates, or piquant with Plato. No more than ten kiddies form a party. They vote on the topic of choice for the day and plunge into profundity with a vengeance.

Our brat in today's gospel reading, aka the prodigal son, also plunges into profundity – but not by choice. He isn't interested in insight, or in grappling with life's mysteries. All he wants are life's pleasures. He gets them, such as they are, and – surprise! surprise! – ends up more miserable than he was before he had them.

Had he developed a taste for philosophical tea he might have fared better. Had he used his head to wise up he would have fared better. We are blessed with the most complex organ in the universe. It's called a brain. Surprising how long it takes for some to find it.

TWENTY-FIFTH SUNDAY IN ORDINARY TIME

Readings: Amos 8:4-7; 1 Timothy 2:1-8; Luke 16:1-13

Little Things Mean a Lot

Somebody described a diamond as a lump of coal that did well under pressure. Not so for dandelion seeds. Under pressure, recently, they caused problems. A train travelling from Halifax, West Yorkshire to King's Cross, London, had its engines clogged by drifting dandelion seeds. These spindly, puffy parachutes blocked the air filters in four of its five engines. The mighty machine could only inch ignominiously into King's Cross station.

Even more troublesome were the grains of fine ash from Iceland's Eyjafjallajökull volcano. Consisting of pulverized rock and glass, such ash can wreak havoc on planes. Sandblasting windscreens, they effectively 'blind' pilots. They pit fuselages, damage landing lights, and clog sensors making air speed indicators unreliable. Being charged particles, they disrupt radio communication and even cause power failure. None of these pitted pellets of rock and glass is more than 2 millimetres in diameter. As the song says: little things mean a lot.

Had the manager in today's gospel known that, he might have been more careful with his employer's property. Caught in the mire of cheating, he sinks deeper into scheming and theft. Anyone crooked enough to go along with his dishonest ruse could hardly be relied upon to come to his help at a later date. Why should they? Honour among thieves? I doubt it.

When life's worries weigh us down, let's remember the lump of coal. Pressure transformed it. It can transform us too. We're already halfway there when we remember, if not the diamond then, the pearl of great price we carry within us: God's Holy Spirit.

TWENTY-SIXTH SUNDAY IN ORDINARY TIME

Readings: Amos 6:1, 4-7; 1 Timothy 6:11-16; Luke 16:19-31

Leaving it Too Late

The Beano comic book for children used to sell in its early days for 2d. That's two pennies in old currency. Recently an edition of the first annual, from 1939, sold for £4,264. It was one of only 11 copies believed to be in existence. Just goes to show that what seems of little value today may be quite valuable tomorrow. It's good to prize things now, rather than regret later, perhaps.

That's certainly true of the rich man in today's gospel. He didn't put much value on Lazarus at his doorstep begging each day. Later, when he sees how important Lazarus is, he comes to realise the error of his ways. But it's too late.

This is not an easy parable to accept. It touches on things dark and deep: the condition of serious sinners after death. While he may not have harmed Lazarus during his lifetime, the rich man's heartless indifference to his plight was evil enough to land him in what we would call hell.

This is an unsettling parable. It's uncompromising in what it says. It poses too many problems to go into here, but it should stop me in my tracks. It's intended to. It forces me to ask questions I may not want to ask, questions that have little interest, immediacy, or value for me today, perhaps. But what about tomorrow? Certainly, one of those questions must be: do I take seriously the consequences of what I do, and don't do?

Is the thought of eternal damnation in any way for me like *The Beano*? Comical.

TWENTY-SEVENTH SUNDAY IN ORDINARY TIME

Readings: Habakkuk 1:2-3, 2.2-4; 2 Timothy 1:6-8, 13-14; Luke 17:5-19

Right Spirit

Made to measure medicine is just around the corner. A corner that's about a decade away, that is. According to the scientist who led the Human Genome Project, most of us in the affluent world will have our genetic codes sequenced by then for less than €800. Knowing our genetic code, a doctor could then prescribe drugs more safely and effectively.

I wonder can a gene affect a soul, or spirit – that part of us that doesn't show up even under the most intense scans, or the most powerful of microscopes? It's strange then that in today's first reading – dating from about 600BC – the prophet Habakkuk could shrewdly note that 'The spirit of the proud is not right in them.' There's something wrong with them; something askew inside them. But I doubt if knowing their DNA sequence would right their spirit.

When it comes to having a right spirit inside us I'd say right parents are needed. A survey by the Catholic Children's Society of the Westminster Diocese reported that on average people give one hour daily to primetime TV shows, but only 49 minutes daily to their children. Some 68 per cent of parents said that their need for money was the reason for giving so little time to their children.

The Catholic Children's Society said that from experience they know that children need relational stability, the self-esteem that comes from feeling valued for who they are and knowing they're loved by their parents.

DNA is undoubtedly important: Deeply Needed Attention, that is.

TWENTY-EIGHTH SUNDAY IN ORDINARY TIME

Readings: 2 Kings 5:14-17; 2 Timothy 2:8-13; Luke 17:11-19

Faith or Prozac

There's something fishy going on in our waters. And it's all to do with drugs. In 2009 in England doctors prescribed 39 million courses of antidepressants. That's a third more than in 2005. After due process, these drugs filter into our waterways and the sea. Effluent concentrates in estuaries and costal regions, the habitat of shrimp and other marine life. Shrimp are ingesting the excreted drugs of whole towns, with depressing results. Instead of swimming away from light and scuttling under rocks, as normally they do, these souped-up specimens swim towards sunlit water and become prey for passing fish. By feeding on fluoxetine – the active chemical in Prozac – they are five times more likely to swim towards the light. This harms the ecosystem's delicate balance.

In light of that, today's gospel is of particular interest, especially Jesus' statement: 'Get up and go on your way; your faith has made you well.' It would be very interesting to have a breakdown on those 39 million prescriptions. One wonders how many were for people of no faith.

While faith alone doesn't heal the lepers in today's gospel, it does bring them to the source of health: Jesus. Clearly, one can't simply link the presence of illness with an absence of faith. But it's well to remember that faith doesn't serve pie-in-the-sky. It instils a healthy attitude of hope towards the future. But also it enables us to cope with things now. For some people that might be a more bitter pill to swallow than Prozac.

TWENTY-NINTH SUNDAY IN ORDINARY TIME

Readings: Exodus 17:8-13; 2 Timothy 3:14-4:2; Luke 18:1-8

Spiritual 'makeover'

It's one approach to getting people off the dole, but it's controversial. To ease unemployment in the Netherlands three local councils are offering unemployed single women a €1,400 fashion and beauty makeover. The better you look the better your chances, the idea seems to be, of finding a husband or a job. Those chosen for the scheme will also be schooled in the social graces. When the crash course in carrying oneself is completed a professional photograph of the new you will appear on the website of an exclusive dating agency that claims a 75 per cent success rate. However, with over 600 unemployed singles eligible not everyone considers the expense involved as money well spent.

It just goes to show the importance some people attach to outward appearance. Today's second reading, however, doesn't. It presents us with a different set of values – ones concerned with the quality of what's inside a person rather than their skin-deep looks. For a thorough spiritual 'makeover' Paul reminds us there's nothing better than immersion in what he calls the 'sacred writings.'

All scripture is inspired by God, he tells us. And it has many uses. It can teach, correct, reprove, and train in righteousness. It motivates and equips people both to be good and to do good. While this type of spiritual 'makeover' doesn't cost a penny, it doesn't come cheap either. Its cost isn't in euro, but in the currency of faith, hope, love, generosity, kindness, service, and other equally attractive characteristics. Too bad not everybody wants to employ these.

THIRTIETH SUNDAY IN ORDINARY TIME

Readings: Sirach 35:12-14, 16-19; 2 Timothy 4:6-8, 16-18; Luke 9:1-6

The Race

The legendary Greek, Pheidippides, ran the first 'marathon' in 490BC. Running 40km from Marathon to Athens, he brought the good news of Persian defeat. Unfortunately he overdid it and dropped dead. Besides his good-news message, he brought another too – albeit unintended: if you run a marathon, prepare for it. You have to train a lot. You have to sacrifice time and comfort. And you must be able to cope with physical stress and endure pain. Yet each year more than 800 marathons are held worldwide. That means that several hundreds of thousands of people run 42.195km in what is considered to be recreational running.

In today's second reading Paul says that he has fought the good fight and finished the race. Neither is recreational. The distance he covers is not measured in kilometres, miles or any such units. It's measured in terms of spiritual maturity. The 'units' used to measure this 'distance' are: faith, witness and proclamation. His, as ours, is not a race that covers distance. It covers time, and life's experiences both good and bad. It covers advances and retreats, ups and downs, and the about turns we make in life. It covers the 'walls' we face that block our progress to God. It has its highs too: the exhilaration of insight, the thrill of hope's promises, the calm of a clear conscience, the peace of mind from goodness shown, and the security of God's love.

This good news is worth dying for. Paul did so. This is not Greek legend.

THIRTY-FIRST SUNDAY IN ORDINARY TIME

Readings: Wisdom 11:22-12:2; 2 Thessalonians 1:11-2:2; Luke 19:1-10

Home Alone

If there are little green men out there, why haven't we seen any sign of them? They could be big instead of small and blue instead of green, like the Na'vi on Pandora in the sci-fi film *Avatar*. Size and colour don't matter. What does matter is that to date we seem to be the only intelligent life form in this or any neck of the universe. According to recent scientific investigations complex life is rare even in our own galaxy and probably even rarer in other parts of the universe. Like it or not, it seems we're home alone.

That's a scary scenario for some – and would be for all did God not exist. His word in today's first reading expands our mind. It asks us to think big, to embrace the universe and allow the inevitable feeling of wonder to work its magic in our spirit. It tells us that God hates nothing that he has made. What exists is here because he wants it here. As we're still relatively new to the universe, we're still finding these things out. Therefore, an open mind is essential both towards little green men and God alike.

The crowd in today's gospel reading don't have an open mind towards Jesus eating with Zacchaeus, a tax collector and, in their eyes, a sinner. Because of that, they miss out on an important truth: Jesus comes to seek out and save the lost.

What truths do we need to open our minds to so as not to lose out?

THIRTY-SECOND SUNDAY IN ORDINARY TIME

Readings: 2 Maccabees 7:1-2, 9-14; 2 Thessalonians 2:16-3:5; Luke 20:27-38

Gut-feeling

One thing can be said about life: it never ceases to amaze. Take, for example, a decade-long ocean census completed early in 2010. It uncovered a whole new world of a billion marine microbes. That's an incredible 50,000 times more microbes than were known to exist before the census. How much more of life's largesse do we short-change, I wonder.

Do we short-change life's extravagance even in the case of human beings, particularly when a person's earthly life has come to an end? How many are tempted to think, 'Well that's that! *Finito*!' The Jewish sect in today's gospel reading holds such a view. The Sadducees don't believe in life after death. For them there is no such thing as bodily resurrection. Today, lots of people think that way too, or would claim they do. But that's such a bleak outlook to have!

Even were it true, I'd still crave some comfort – even that of delusion – to face the abyss of oblivion. Let delusion cushion the icy impact of eternal emptiness and the sickening thrust of a risible freedom that leads nowhere and to nothing. In such a case one might as well be a robot as a human being.

So much of what we experience each day tells us that life is not a trickster. It tells us that we are players in a drama, not a farce. We can trust our intuitions, our insights and our feelings. There's more ways to truth than through scientific observation and logical reasoning. Let's never forget our gut.

THIRTY-THIRD SUNDAY IN ORDINARY TIME

Readings: Malachy 3:19-20; 2 Thessalonians 3:7-12; Luke 21:5-19

Leaps but no Bounds

Social isolation can damage your health as much as smoking can. According to new research it can be as bad for you as smoking 15 cigarettes a day, or daily binge drinking. It's twice as harmful as being obese. Good relationships are crucial for physical and mental health. This is true not just for the elderly as previously thought but for people of all ages. Those with strong bonds to others are 50 per cent less likely to die over a seven-year period, for example, than those lacking quality relationships. One researcher explains that having a sense of meaning in life helps people to take better care of themselves.

Today's second reading agrees. There, Paul says that we need to earn our bread. In other words, we must pull our weight in working with others for the common good. We don't isolate ourselves emotionally or physically from others. We don't become loafers, spongers or gossips. We remain active, and contribute to the common good. In that way, we remain in good shape – in every sense of the word.

It also means looking out for those who because of circumstances may find themselves either in, or slipping into, social isolation. It means being on the watch so that we never lose our sense of meaning, or because of indifference allow another to lose theirs. In that way we revere God's name in those he created and, as the first reading so charmingly puts it, we go out to face life 'leaping like calves from the stall'.

OUR LORD JESUS CHRIST UNIVERSAL KING

Readings: 2 Samuel 5:1-3; Colossians 1:12-20; Luke 23:35-43

Go Cosmic for Christ

Bye, bye 'ordinary' time. Welcome cosmic. The church's liturgical year ends this week – and with a bang by celebrating Jesus Christ as King of the Universe. And what a universe it is! Its sheer size, astonishing age and confounding complexity are beyond anything our minds can grasp. The more we see of it through the Very Large Telescope in Chile, or the Hubble and Kepler space telescopes, the more awesome it appears.

From data obtained 22,000 light years distant, astronomers have lit upon a new class of star so colossal it shatters current theoretical limits as to how large a star can be. Then, in June, 2010 in just one download of information, the Kepler telescope doubled the number of known planets outside our solar system to 700. Just as scientists realise through their impressive discoveries how little they know compared to what can be known, so too should we as people of faith realise the same as far as our faith is concerned.

Dogmas don't close doors. They ensure that the right doors are opened. The door to the cosmic Christ is clearly marked in today's second reading. There we have the risen Christ described as the one in whom 'all things in heaven and on earth were created' – even these newly discovered colossal stars, and all things as yet undetected by human technology.

There's more to faith than morals. There's the breathtaking, visionary, near cockeyed, mind-stretching promise of a fullness of life beyond death that no telescope could ever reveal. That's what faith is for. Happy New Year!

ST PATRICK' DAY: YEAR A

Readings: Sirach 39:6-10; 2 Timothy 4:1-8; Matthew 13:24-32

No Hiding Place

God makes a habit of choosing the wrong people for the job. In the Old Testament he appoints Jeremiah as a 'prophet to the nations'. Jeremiah objects strongly. Says he can't speak well and is too immature for such a demanding job. Then, in the New Testament Jesus sends 70 followers on ahead of him to the towns he will visit later. He sends them as 'lambs into the midst of wolves'. How weird! Who else could disregard best practice like that and get away with it?

Who could have predicted that a worldwide faith community would eventually form from that mustard seed referred to in today's gospel reading – that smallest of all seeds, sown by a few lambs among many wolves? No one. God chooses people who have little or nothing to offer by way of skills and abilities simply because he doesn't need them. What he wants is a generous and sincere heart. That's more than enough to work with.

He called unskilled fishermen and look what happened. He called Patrick, an unskilled shepherd and look what happened. He's deaf to objections, and blind to limitations.

Like the TV Licence Inspector, he's heard all the excuses. None of them works. When God calls there is nowhere to hide. And why would one want to?

ST PATRICK'S DAY: YEAR B

Readings: Jeremiah 1:4-9; 2 Timothy 4:1-8; Mark 16:15-20

Camel Knot

Desert wisdom tells us: 'Trust in God, but tie your camel to a tree.' Its wry humour notwithstanding, it is sad advice. Clearly from today's alternative second reading, Paul would shun it. He has complete trust in God. He doesn't need, and doesn't have, a Plan B. So trusting is he that he sounds boastful, even presumptuous – until we remember the God he believes in: he who is merciful, gracious, slow to anger, abounding in mercy and steadfast love (Ps 103:8).

That's our God too. Or is it? Would we dare claim, as Paul does, that we fight the good fight, keep the faith and await the crown of righteousness reserved for us? Somehow, I think not. We'd be afraid that God would be angry with us. Strangely, even perversely, it's often those who expend themselves the most for God who show the least confidence in his steadfast love. One wonders what drives them: love, or fear.

There's no false modesty in what Paul claims today, no low self-esteem. Neither is there pride, or arrogance, or an inflated ego. There's simply the confidence of a mature man that what he has done is pleasing to God, and that God will acknowledge that when the time comes. Could anything be more natural?

Any less gracious image of God is a distortion, and at odds with what St Patrick – whom we commemorate today – brought us. With a whimsical god you need a camel knot. But with our God you don't need to get into a knot – ever!

ST PATRICK'S DAY: YEAR C

Readings: Amos 7:12-15; 1 Thessalonians 2:2-8; Luke 5:1-11

Driving You Nuts!

It's enough to drive you nuts. Only conkers marked with a special fluorescent pen to prevent cheating may be used at the smash-hit Poulton International Conkers Tournament in Gloucestershire. This ensures that the coveted conkers haven't been battle-hardened by soaking in vinegar or by baking in an oven. 'Is nothing sacred?' I hear you ask.

Saint Patrick wouldn't have had to ask that question. Lots of things and places were sacred then: stone circles, passage tombs, dolmens, oghams, fires, and of course mountain tops.

The place where Jesus calls his first disciples in today's gospel reading is sacred too, if unusual. A sacred place is where we meet God, be it the resplendent Barque of Peter, or Simon's simple boat. The totally unexpected and incredibly heavy catch of fish points to something mysterious at work. So much so, that Peter falls on his knees before Jesus in awe and fear.

We, however, carry God around within us and think nothing of it. We believe in the indwelling of the Holy Spirit. A legacy of faith from St Patrick, it's beyond price. It roots the realisation in us that God is incredibly close, and not only because we're holy (which we are) but also because we're sinners (which we are).

That fact of faith may be enough to drive some people nuts too. Marked for God, we can never use sin – our own or others – as an excuse to distance ourselves from him. No cheap fluorescent pen marks us. God is closer to us than we are to ourselves.

THE ASSUMPTION OF THE BLESSED VIRGIN MARY: YEAR A

Readings: Apocalypse 11:19, 12:1-6; 1 Corinthians 15:20-26; Luke 1:39-56

That Leap

There's a detail in today's gospel reading that always intrigues me. It's the child in Elizabeth's womb leaping for joy at the sound of Mary's greeting. Not the sort of detail fiction writers normally come up with. When you consider the event through the eyes of faith, however, it makes great sense. Mary, pregnant with the source of life, visits her cousin, Elizabeth, whose pregnancy is the gift of divine promise. Saying so spontaneously that the child in her womb leaps for joy at Mary's greeting, conveys graphically how extraordinary the 'Presence' is that Mary hosts in her womb.

The extraordinariness is evident even before the birth. There are exceptional circumstances surrounding the conception described in terms of angelic annunciation and overshadowing by God's Spirit. But even before that, we believe Mary was conceived immaculate. Again, in faith this makes great sense, and is most appropriate, perhaps even imperative. Now, the life force of that resulting child asserts itself beyond physical confines. Being close to the source of life quickens.

Do we ever get the surge, feel ourselves being quickened by God's presence? It won't make us leap and jump for joy, but it will bring vigour and freshness to our lives as we await the fulfilment of God's promise that the best is yet to come.

The event we celebrate today points to this. So inappropriate is it that she who was conceived immaculate should experience death's decay, that on 1 November 1950 Pope Pius XII defined as divinely revealed that Mary was assumed 'body and soul into heavenly glory'.

THE ASSUMPTION OF THE BLESSED VIRGIN MARY: YEAR B

Readings: Apocalypse 11:19, 12:1-6, 10; 1 Corinthians 15:20-26; Luke 1:39-56

Inside out

Teilhard de Chardin wrote in *Hymn of the Universe*, 'Continue to regard man as an accidental out-growth or sport of nature and you will drive him into a state of disgust or revolt which, if it became general, would mean the definitive stoppage of life on earth.' That's a crucial comment.

If we deny the reality of things we don't have empirical evidence for, are we not confining human intelligence within narrow parameters? When a physicist predicts the existence of a subatomic particle using a mathematical formula, but has to wait until someone empirically establishes its existence before he receives the Nobel Prize, that doesn't mean he was talking through his mathematical hat until then. He was correct, but no one could prove it outside of maths.

Something similar applies to Mary's assumption. Using a faith formula, the church teaches, 'We pronounce, declare, and define it to be a divinely revealed dogma: that the Immaculate Mother of God, the ever Virgin Mary, having completed the course of her earthly life, was assumed body and soul into heavenly glory.' (#44 Apostolic Constitution of Pope Pius XII, *Munificentissimus Deus*). However, there the analogy ends. There's no way to empirically establish the truth of that statement short of a Marian apparition to confirm it. Even then, Doubting Thomases would abound.

Today's feast reminds me of what Richard Rohr states in *Things Hidden*: 'Spirituality basically teaches us that the inside of things is bigger than the outside.' There's more to life than meets the eye. I hope that's not an assumption equally difficult to accept.

THE ASSUMPTION OF THE BLESSED VIRGIN MARY YEAR C

Readings: Apocalypse 11:19, 12:1-6, 10; 1 Corinthians 15:20-26; Luke 1:39-56

Test of Faith

This feast really is a test of faith. Today's first and second readings don't make things any easier. I suppose for many it's just a feast and that's it. Just something we commemorate because the church teaches infallibly that it happened. Interestingly, she says nothing about how it happened but asserts that it did. I think this feast should not be seen as an isolated event. If today's readings are telling us anything it's that the event we commemorate is part of a grand plan unfolding.

The first reading from the Apocalypse, using what for us at this distance is very strange imagery, tells of the conflict between good and evil. We can all identify with that to some degree as we experience this tug-of-war on a daily basis in our own lives. The purpose of this reading and its weird symbols is not to tell us that such conflict occurs – we know that already – but that the outcome is assured: victory for the good. That is not something we may know already, or always experience. We may be duped at times into thinking that evil is more powerful than good. How wrong we would be should we think that way. Today's feast should help to convince us of that.

So too should our second reading from Paul: 'The last enemy to be destroyed is death.' Mary did not undergo death as we know it, according to church teaching. She did not undergo bodily corruption. In Jesus' resurrection, the perceived finality of death has been shattered.

THE FEAST OF ALL SAINTS: YEAR A

Readings: Apocalypse 7:2-2, 9-14; 1 John 3:1-3; Matthew 5:1-12

Stranger than Fiction

I was a closet 'trekkie'. While I don't hyperdrive into flights of fantasy anymore, I'm still intrigued by science fiction's portrayal of extra-terrestrials. Usually they look like mutants. Their form, even when almost human, is degraded. Even ones posturing as 'superior' have bizarre characteristics.

The world's greatest artists fare no better when it comes to giving an imagined superior being a form that's superior to our own. For example, artists resort to portraying angels as humans with wings, and cumbersome ones at that.

Today's second reading doesn't try to turn fact into fiction. John states simply 'What we will be has not yet been revealed. What we do know is this: when he is revealed, we will be like him.'

On the feast of All Saints we celebrate something that's stranger than fiction. 'Strange' deriving from the Latin *extraneus* means 'external'. What we believe, truly is external to fiction. It's as far from fiction as you can get. And that is fact.

We believe that a destiny awaits us – one that's wonderful beyond imagining. It's open to all people of good will. Scripture tells us that the human eye has not seen, nor the human ear heard, nor has it entered the mind of man what things God has prepared for those who love him.

Were we to ask God to beam us up to catch a glimpse of it we could never be happy again with earth as we know it. Wisely, we're to journey in faith, not trek in starry-eyed fantasy.

THE FEAST OF ALL SAINTS: YEAR B

Readings: Apocalypse 7:2-4, 9-14; 1 John 3:1-3; Matthew 5:1-12

Back to the Future

The year 2009 marked the 150th anniversary of the publication of Charles Darwin's book, *The Origin of Species*. Many scientists today accept that there is a huge body of evidence supporting the view that we have descended from an animal with chimpanzee-like capacities. If we have, then what we hear today's first reading telling us is all the more amazing. For there we have attained near god-like capacities.

Which is more difficult to believe: that a crude chimp is now a sophisticated human who composes sublime symphonies, produces fabulous works of art, explores cosmic vastness and penetrates atomic depths; or to believe that this human is destined for near divinity in a new ordering of creation?

Science serves truth in dull and detailed prose. Scripture sets it in sweeping story and inspiring imagery that lift us higher than science can ever do. Science examines and reports. Scripture reveals and inspires. Science fixes us firmly to matter; scripture frees us as spirit.

Saints – all of them – are the poets among us. Not *vice versa,* though. They are what the old pop song jingles out, 'poetry in motion'. As poetry opens pathways to understanding, refines human emotions, and grants glimpses of transcendence we would not otherwise experience, so saints have done and continue to do through the generosity and sanctity of their lives. They show us what life can be like because of what it will be like. They bring the future to our doorstep.

Whether we grant it entrance to our home is up to us.

FEAST OF ALL SAINTS YEAR C

Readings: Apocalypse 7:2-4, 9-14; 1 John 3:1-3; Matthew 5:1-12

Hard-wired for Beauty

Babies come beautifully bundled for life. Even from day one they can recognise numbers. They know, very basically, the difference between one, two and many. For example, when shown a card with one dot over and over again, eventually they get bored and look away. But then, if shown one with two dots their interest is aroused again. And these bundles of joy can recognise simple groups of musical notes that they have heard before at some stage.

But, most intriguing of all, some scientists think that babies are born with an ingrained sense of beauty. They arrive at that conclusion from the fact that newborn babies stare longer at attractive faces than at unattractive ones. Scientists think that babies do this because an attractive face is closer to the standard human face that babies are hard-wired to recognise.

Beauty is what saints hard-wire themselves to recognise and follow all their lives: the ultimate beauty of God himself, and the beauty that his presence in all people, places and things radiates. But perhaps above all else saints commit themselves to the beauty of a life lived well, a life concerned with truth, honesty, generosity; a life showing respect and concern for others, a life inspired by faith in a good God and strengthened by hope in his promise of everlasting life in all its fullness.

Today we celebrate 'the great multitude' mentioned in our first reading and indeed the multitudes of every generation who, falling in love with beauty, have and do sacrifice all things for him.